MU

Jeremy Josephs ... called to the Bar ... at Bordeaux Univ..... became political assistant to the Rt Hon Sir David Steel, MP, the then leader of the Liberal Party. He is the author of *Inside the Alliance*, *Swastika Over Paris*, *Dr Jack: Calcutta's Pavement Doctor*, which formed the basis of an Everyman television documentary in 1993 and *Hungerford: One Man's Massacre*. Jeremy Josephs now lives with his wife and two children in Montpellier, France, where he teaches at the university's Faculty of Law.

Also by Jeremy Josephs:

Inside the Alliance
Swastika Over Paris
Dr Jack: Calcutta's Pavement Doctor
Hungerford: One Man's Massacre

Murder in the Family

The Inside Story of the Jersey Murders

Jeremy Josephs

HEADLINE

Distributed by
Trafalgar Square
North Pomfret, Vermont 05053

First published in 1994
by HEADLINE BOOK PUBLISHING

10 9 8 7 6 5 4 3 2 1

ISBN 0 7472 4455 3

Typeset by
Letterpart Limited, Reigate, Surrey

Printed and bound in Great Britain by
Cox & Wyman Ltd, Reading, Berks

HEADLINE BOOK PUBLISHING
A division of Hodder Headline PLC
338 Euston Road
London NW1 3BH

Contents

Acknowledgements

Blame Arthur Frank! For it was my father-in-law who suggested that I should write a book about the Newall case. He put the idea to me not once but at least a dozen times. And now I see why he was so insistent, for this book has proved to be extremely fascinating both to research and write. This appalling story has captured the imagination not just of Jersey men and women but of people all over the world. I hope that I have done justice to both its intricacies and its sheer horror.

I am indebted to many people for their help in the writing of this book – so many that I shall simply list their names rather than attempt to specify the precise manner in which each was of assistance. I would like therefore to express my gratitude and appreciation to Jimmy Adamson, Angela Barnes, Julian Bernstein, Michael Blackey, Alan Brooke, Catherine Buddin,

Charles Canham, Alister Clark, Nancy Clark, Nick Cooper, Paolo Corolla, Richard Dawes, David Ellam, Maureen Ellam, Rachel Ellison, Martin Farley, Natividade Ferreira, Martin Fitzgerald, David Frank, Julie Frank, Sandra Genee, Kate Hall, Frank Hayes, Celia Kent, Bob Le Breton, David Le Quesne, Terry MacDonald, Charles MacDowall, Paul Marks, George Marshman, Jack Merrivale, Stephen Newall, Graham Nimmo, Sergio Parmesan, Philip Perree, Alan Phillips, Philippa Richardson, Barry Simpson, Irene Stevenson, Pat Stoker, Corinne Symonds, Nicholas Symonds and Barry Wilkinson. I would also like to thank all members of both the Josephs and Symonds families. And finally, thank you, Arthur, too.

Jeremy Josephs
June 1994

Murder in the
Family

1

'The Best Marriage
I Have Ever Seen'

Another couple of months and it would be five years.
Five years since the night he had beaten his parents to
death with a Chinese rice-flail, lacerating their skulls
and drenching their Jersey bungalow with blood. Five
years of freedom for Roderick Newall; five years of
frustration for the island's police. No wonder he had
begun to believe that he had got away with it. The
bodies of Nicholas and Elizabeth Newall had been
buried so efficiently that, despite the most intensive
police search ever conducted in Jersey's history, they
had never been found. No bodies. No motive. No
arrest. The perfect double murder.

Matters might have rested there had the Newalls'
elder son been able to hold his tongue. But his
overwhelming sense of guilt had betrayed him. Now,
on the afternoon of 5 August 1992, aboard HMS

Argonaut, a hundred and fifty miles south-west of Gibraltar, he was about to pay the price for having unburdened himself so freely. For the States of Jersey police, more accustomed to dealing with drunks and shoplifters, had enlisted the help of the Royal Navy and the Gibraltar police in bringing Roderick Newall to justice.

Believing that his papers were to be routinely inspected, Newall had agreed to leave his ocean-going yacht, the *Austral Soma*, and rowed the short distance to the Leander-class frigate. As he did so, five armed officers of the Royal Gibraltar Police got ready to file out from where they were hiding. Once he was on board, they enclosed him in a semicircle, his back to the sea.

'Boy,' the fugitive yachtsman was informed, 'have we got a surprise for you.'

The Newall family loved the sea, and a quarter of a century earlier, when he set sail for the West Indies, Nicholas Newall had every reason to feel proud. Everything was going according to plan. The many months of meticulous planning and preparation appeared to have paid off. Now the islands of Jamaica, Cuba and Haiti beckoned. How refreshing, the thirty-six-year-old skipper of *Rodmark* thought, to be away from Scotland and the world of prep-school teaching. Nor had the constraints of family life been able to thwart his project in any way, for pottering around on deck were two tiny but extremely boisterous souls, Roderick and Mark, aged three years and eighteen months respectively. Two sets of eyes had been scrutinizing the Newall boys' every move: those of their mother Elizabeth and their Scottish nanny.

Envied by family and friends alike, the Newalls were aware of how privileged they were to be setting off in fulfilment of a dream. But rather than heading out towards the North Atlantic and the Azores, Nicholas Newall soon found himself charting a much more modest course, pointing his yacht towards the harbour of St Helier, Jersey, instead. The tiny island clearly enchanted the Newalls, just as it had worked its magic on Queen Victoria one hundred and twenty years earlier, for their Caribbean expedition, scarcely under way, was abruptly abandoned there and then.

Elizabeth Newall was adamant that everyone should ignore her seasickness, to which she had long been accustomed. But the youngest sailor on board, Mark, had been ill for much of the crossing from England, blacking out on more than one occasion. His parents did not require a doctor's opinion to know that their son was in no fit state to complete the more arduous journey into the heavier seas of the Atlantic. For what if he should suddenly require urgent medical attention or specialist paediatric care? What on earth would they do then?

It was such thoughts that had made Nicholas Newall realize that he was unlikely to follow in the wash of Christopher Columbus and the *Santa Maria* after all – at least not for the time being. Vowing that one day his ambitious project would become a reality, he made his way instead to a branch of Barclays Bank in St Helier to withdraw some sterling, a currency he had not been

3

expecting to need for some time. There he also sought advice on a good hotel. What he did not know, however, as he attended to these unscheduled affairs, was that Jersey was destined to become the Newall family's home for the next twenty years.

The Newalls had set foot on a beautiful but strange little island. Sometimes referred to as the Queen of the Channel, because of its majestic coastline and country-side, Jersey is not really in the English Channel at all. It is in fact in the Bay of St Malo, and therefore very near France. Neither a sovereign state nor a colonial dependency, the island is most certainly British, while at the same time not an integral part of the United Kingdom. Anomalies and anachronisms abound. Islanders retain their own language yet English is spoken by all. They have their own banknotes but trade in pounds at all times. Elections are held regularly and contested with great gusto, but party politics is notice-able only by its absence. Stylish and sporty cars appear from each and every direction, yet nowhere does the speed limit exceed forty miles an hour. But for all the island's baffling idiosyncrasies and quirks of history, Nicholas and Elizabeth Newall realized right away that they had stumbled on a truly delightful spot. A histo-rian by training, Nicholas Newall soon read what Queen Victoria had had to say on the subject. Visiting the island in 1846, she found that St Aubin's Bay reminded her of Naples. 'What a pretty, rich place this is,' she had declared – a judgement with which both Nicholas and Elizabeth wholeheartedly concurred.

Yet things had apparently not always been so cosy on the island. For the *Penny Cyclopaedia*, published shortly after the turn of that century had reported in far less glowing terms:

High winds are prevalent and violent gales frequently blow. The predominant diseases are rheumatism, liver complaints, indigestion and intermittent fevers. The common diet among the farmers and country people is 'soupe à choux', [containing] lard and potatoes; sometimes, but rarely, a little meat is added. Cider is the common drink. This meagre diet has probably contributed to a deterioration of the inhabitants both in stature and appearance.

Jersey must have seen a rapid recovery indeed, for by the time the Newalls arrived in 1967 they could find only an equable climate, rude health and good food. They decided to make the island their home, and bought Martello Cottage at St Brelade. The bay to the south is one of Jersey's most beautiful, well known for its red granite cliffs, sheltered slopes and long beaches of perfect, golden sands. The Newalls congratulated themselves on their decision. It was true that they had been obliged to abandon their adventure; true too that a few folk in Scotland had scoffed and smirked. But in choosing to settle on such an agreeable island had they not fallen on their feet after all?

Elizabeth had met the man who was to become her

husband while teaching at New Park Preparatory School in St Andrews, a city once known as the ecclesiastical capital of Scotland. Nicholas, nine years her senior, was already an established teacher there when Elizabeth arrived as an eager new recruit, fresh from teacher training college. She was already engaged to another man, Mike Hill, a junior doctor with an affable, easygoing personality and who fitted in with her family exceedingly well. Their romance had blossomed some years earlier, when they were students at St Andrews University, the oldest seat of learning in Scotland, having been founded in the fifteenth century. Elizabeth had read modern languages while Mike was studying for his doctorate in medicine. As soon as Nicholas Newall had appeared on the scene, however, she could not break off her engagement quickly enough. Nicholas, she announced, was the man she really loved; it was a judgement in which she would not waver. This time, however, her family's approval of her choice of partner was not quite so forthcoming.

'When we first met Nick,' Elizabeth's sister, Nan Clark, would later explain:

We weren't terribly enamoured or enthusiastic at all. He was a very odd person. He seemed to be completely unsuitable for my sister – he didn't have the same enthusiasms as her. I felt that having met him she almost began to play-act a certain role in life. She was no longer the Elizabeth I knew. She seemed to me to adapt to the role of the wife in the Enid Blyton books, with Nick as the gruff, almost detached husband. She would do everything to accommodate Nick, to fit in with him, to pursue his interests rather than hers, whereas she had so much potential of her own.

Nor, for that matter, were the Newall elders keen on the match. Well connected within the world of freemasonry and with senior members of the Scottish judiciary, they considered Elizabeth's family, the Nelsons, to be considerably beneath them in social class. But every attempt to sabotage their relationship proved to be not only ill-fated but also counterproductive. When, therefore, it became obvious that the couple were edging inevitably towards matrimony, both families began to reconcile themselves to the match and the prospect of an impending marriage. Thus it was that in 1963, as the Newall and Nelson clans both did their best to stifle frowns and prevent eyebrows from rising spontaneously in a last-minute display of disapproval, Nicholas and Elizabeth were wed. Eros must have smiled broadly that day, for the match was undoubtedly a triumph for love.

Throughout their marriage it was never an easy task to produce people prepared to put in a good word for Nicholas Newall. Even Maureen Ellam, who was to become one of his closest confidants in later life, had a habit of referring to her friend as a pompous pig, although she was of course always quick to qualify that remark. 'It was true that more people disliked him than liked him,' she explains. 'But once you got in behind

7

that rather arrogant façade you had an absolutely delightful friend for life.'

Nicholas Newall had had a very deprived childhood. Not that there had ever been any shortage of money; quite the contrary, for material things were seldom in short supply. The Newalls were an old Scottish industrial family who, at the turn of the century, had built up a respectable fortune on the west coast. The enterprise, although profitable, was far from glamorous: the sprawling works near Rhu in Strathclyde, overlooking Gare Loch, manufactured nuts and bolts for the booming shipbuilding industry. Nevertheless it provided the wherewithal to send Nicholas, together with Stephen, his identical twin, to Loretto, at Musselburgh, which is considered to be the finest public school in Scotland.

Money was never an issue; it was rather that Nicholas was denied a love that should rightfully have been his. But both parents had been so involved with one another that they had little time or energy for either of their twin sons. In fact they were very often not present at all, preferring to spend their time together on holiday, away from Scotland. As a result, the boys spent the best part of their formative years being pushed from pillar to post. During those key years of childhood their circuit repeated itself time and again: either they were being cared for by a nanny, or they were away at boarding school, or, much of the time, they would while away the hours in the company of their paternal grandparents.

This taste of extended family life scarcely compensated for the lack of proper parenting and care. In fact it compounded their problems, stifling their development still further. For their grandfather was a very odd character. One of his own children, Kenneth, uncle to the twins, was an exceptionally small man – so much so that he was permanently barred from appearing in his father's presence. Nor had grandfather Newall ever sought to disguise the reason for this cruel banishment. It could hardly have been more straightforward: he was simply repulsed by the sight of his own son. A callous and bad-tempered man, with a reputation for extreme swings of mood, he was the person who played the dominant role in Nicholas's upbringing. Is it really surprising, then, that in later life Nicholas experienced emotional difficulties of his own? Had it not been inevitable that eventually he would struggle to express himself in the unfamiliar language of love?

An excellent schooling had provided Nicholas with one thing, however: a fine speaking voice. And he had soon come to realize that this was something which he might well be able to use to his advantage. Rich and creamy in tone, and with only a faint hint of Scots in the background, it was all the more valuable in that Nicholas had always been rather good with words. 'His speech used to remind me of the Poet Laureate Ted Hughes,' Maureen Ellam recalls. 'He would think carefully about what he wanted to say, and this appealed to me a great deal. I remember that my husband once installed a new door in our lounge. "Ah Maureen," Nicholas purred, "I see you are going for optimum view." '

But more often than not Nicholas would use his

9

tongue sharply, his tone often arrogant and condescending. 'I don't know why he was rude to people so often,' his sister-in-law, Nan Clark, confesses.

Maybe this was a way of protecting himself, so that he wouldn't get hurt. And yet if he set his mind to it he could be a wonderful host or guest. At a dinner party, though, if he happened to take a dislike to a particular person, he would just be offensive to them. With me things worked out rather differently. I think that he must have come to realize that he could say pretty much what he liked and I still wasn't going to fall out with him, because he was my sister's husband and that was that. I did come to appreciate Nick more over the years, but I have to say that I never really warmed to him as such. He was too much within himself; too busy looking down on the whole of human nature, sneering and jeering at humanity at large. It was him and them.

Nicholas's Uncle Kenneth eventually retired to the remote island of Sark, not so very far from Jersey, and one of the last bastions of European feudalism. Local dairy farmer Philip Perree, a Sark man born and bred, has reason to remember Nicholas's arrival on the island one day. He had come to visit the diminutive Kenneth, who never did succeed in finding himself a wife. 'Nick was just so stuck-up,' Perree recalls. 'I hadn't seen him for two or three years and simply called out: "Hello Nick" – hardly a crime, you would have thought. To

which he simply barked out in reply: "Mr Newall to
you." I thought to myself, right, that's the last time I'm
having anything to do with you.'

Nicholas might not have known how to handle
people, but he certainly knew all about boats. Indeed
he was never happier than when at sea, and his library
overflowed with books on sailing, rowing and naviga-
tion, with nautical almanacs and tales of seafaring.

Once established in Jersey, Nicholas had continued
to teach, although his heart had never really been in it.
He was nevertheless employed at a number of schools
on the island, including Moorestown, St Michael's, Le
Rocquier and St George's. Whenever the family's
finances required it, he would offer his services as a
teacher. Yet even within the ranks of his own profes-
sion, Nicholas was, as ever, aloof and alone. Barry
Wilkinson remembers him well:

I taught with Nick at St George's – a small prep
school on the island. He was always stand-offish
and dour and not at all well liked in the staff room.
A typical Scot, if you ask me. Rather than teaching
the children, he inflicted education upon them. He
was a stern teacher and a strong disciplinarian. We
knew that he wasn't in the same financial bracket
as the run-of-the-mill schoolteacher – that he was
just filling in. He kept himself to himself. We
didn't expect him to participate in the social life of
the school and he did not.

In fact Nicholas considered himself to be an accomplished

author, and although he battled unsuccessfully to be published, this did not prevent him from writing a number of novels. While these were not intended to be biographical, there seemed to be a striking resemblance between some of Nicholas's own experiences and those of his fictional characters. One novel told the story of a Scottish schoolmaster who married the matron in a boy's prep school, only to pause a while before going on to murder her. Another concerned the subject of twins whose home was in Jersey. There then followed a more traditional work, in the form of a play, about Mary Queen of Scots, whose unwise marital and political actions provoked rebellion in her own country, forcing her to flee to England, where she was eventually beheaded as a Roman Catholic threat to the throne.

Nicholas would often carry out extensive research before putting pen to paper. Writing was a solitary occupation which suited him well, and with the years his style began to improve. Certainly that was the view of family and friends on whom he would occasionally inflict his literary efforts. Yet he never succeeded in getting over the first hurdle to being published, for he regularly sent sample material to the editors of a number of London houses, only to have it rejected. He did manage, however, to have a number of articles published in magazines such as *History Today* and *The Countryman*. But since these were always strictly non-fiction, Nicholas remained deeply disappointed at his inability to persuade publishers to accept his more imaginative work. When Nan Clark asked him why he did not merge his historical research with fiction in order to express himself more effectively, his reply was typically haughty and offhand. 'Because,' the frustrated author replied, 'that would really be prostituting my art.'

Back problems and a rare blood disorder undoubtedly did nothing to improve Nicholas Newall's outlook on life. A calculating and remote man, he appeared to be so out of touch with the world of emotions that very few things seemed capable of upsetting him. Even when someone he knew passed away, he would not allow their demise to trouble him unduly. Displaying not even the slightest sign of grief, he would simply proceed with the job in hand, as if nothing extraordinary had happened. The coldest of cold fish, he could hardly have been more different from his wife.

'I always got on very well with my sister,' Nan Clark recalls:

> Although like all sisters she was sometimes quite impossible. Since I was the older one by four and a half years I somehow saw it as my duty to keep her calm, because she was always full of fits and starts and odd ideas. Full of life, full of energy and full of enthusiasms – that's Elizabeth. She was one of these people who would always make a room much brighter once she had come into it.

Maureen Ellam agrees. She also admired Elizabeth's zest for life:

> She would breeze into my home bubbling with

13

energy, full of it. 'Well,' she would always begin, 'what *do* you think . . .?' She was a big, Amazonian woman, and very beautiful with it. I would often kid her that she was like an overgrown school girl in many ways.

But as jolly as she undoubtedly could be, Elizabeth Newall had a fierce temper which would sometimes get the better of her. Her sister Nan always insisted that it was directly attributable to her full head of red hair. Whatever its origin, witnessing all five feet ten of her in a towering rage was not a particularly edifying sight, for she would seem to momentarily take leave of her senses. When she was beside herself with fury, her normally fresh and freckled complexion appeared to metamorphose into something much more menacing. And although the years taught her the art of knowing when and how to hold her tongue, there was no shortage of occasions when the sparks would fly.

One technique which Elizabeth knew she could always rely on to help was to burn off surplus energy through sport. Tennis seemed to work best of all. An accomplished all-rounder, from her earliest days she had excelled in many other sports too, including golf and badminton. She had once astounded her parents by casually announcing that she had been named captain of the school cricket team. There had been a short period of silence as they paused to remind themselves that their daughter was attending an all-girls school.

For Elizabeth life held few greater pleasures than

popping round to her friend Angela Barnes, one of Jersey's wealthier residents, after a good game of tennis. There she would begin to relax, catching up on local gossip and quietly passing the time of day over a glass or two of wine. This routine would often be repeated four or five times a week. Angela had come to know Elizabeth's requirements well and would always have a bottle of wine chilled, ready and waiting. Sporty and health-conscious though she was, alcohol played an important part in Elizabeth's life. On one occasion when dining together with Nicholas at the Barnes's stylish house, Le Clos de Hugh, in the parish of St John, the Newalls managed to get through two bottles of white wine before lunch, two bottles of red wine during the meal, and then rounded it off with two bottles of good-quality port after dessert. And they could make equally short work of both sherry and beer.

Elizabeth had herself been sent off to boarding school at a relatively early age. Just as her husband's school was considered to be the very best in Scotland for boys, so too was St Leonard's, at St Andrews, regarded as the first choice for girls. There she had thrived, making friends easily and fitting in well, her energy and enthusiasm infectious as always. Having gone on to obtain a master's degree at St Andrews, she was flattered to be offered a scholarship at Cambridge, but decided to turn it down. Preferring to go on to Edinburgh University, she completed her studies by gaining a diploma in teaching and education. It seemed as if she could turn her hand to almost anything – from sport to academic studies. A compulsive telephoner with a soft spot for older people, Elizabeth had a refreshingly simple philosophy: life is for living, and living to the full.

After a few years at St Brelade, in their house near the prestigious Hotel L'Horizon, the Newalls moved into a new home, Crow's Nest, which could scarcely have been named more appropriately. Perched high above the Prince of Wales Hotel at Grève de Lecq and tucked away on the rugged north coast, it boasts one of the most stunning and panoramic views on the island, looking out towards Sark and the sharp-toothed rocks of the Paternosters. But however delightful the scenery outside, the inside of Crow's Nest did not complement its idyllic setting. One who had good reason to know its interior rather well was Natividade Ferreira, a Madeiran woman who cleaned for the Newalls. Elizabeth always called her Natty, while Nicholas chose not to speak to her at all. She recalls that a visit to Grève de Lecq meant hard work indeed:

Crow's Nest really did not look all that nice. It was a very old house and needed a lot of work and repairs. And Mrs Newall was not a very tidy person, so when I used to go over there to tidy and clean once a week it was always in a terrible mess. I was originally only going to work for Mrs Newall for about three or four weeks. But I liked her a lot because she was always very kind and nice to me. So I decided to stay on. She was happy and generous and very clever too. But I did not like Mr Newall though. I always felt as if he was looking down at me. In fact he used to ignore me altogether. He couldn't get out of my way quickly enough, always rushing off to read or write. He was so very different to Mrs Newall.

Natty had hit the nail on the head. How could Nicholas and Elizabeth possibly be suited to one another, with their vastly different temperaments and personalities? And yet, paradoxically, theirs was an extremely close partnership. There was undeniably a chemistry between them which must have eluded all but the most perceptive. Even Nan Clark, who had never really taken to her brother-in-law at all, is forced to admit that it was a thriving and vibrant relationship:

> They loved each other. There was no doubt about that. Elizabeth made sure that the marriage worked. She adapted herself to have much in common with him. She gave up golf, more or less, and took up sailing – Nick's passion of course. She did everything he wanted her to do.

Maureen Ellam is far less restrained in her praise. From the very first time she met the Newalls she was never in any doubt. Here were two individuals completely and utterly devoted to one another. She could therefore state, without the slightest hesitation: 'It was without doubt the best marriage that I have ever seen.'

Angela Barnes offers a different perspective. Unlike Maureen Ellam, who was a relative latecomer into the lives of Elizabeth and Nicholas, she had been able to observe the Newalls at close quarters for some twenty years. 'They led dramatic lives,' she says. 'They lived their lives to the full. And I admired them for it. Good luck to them, I used to say. But in doing so they became very selfish as a couple. Because their approach was to say not just to hell with the kids, but to hell with everybody else as well.'

In fact Nicholas had not wanted to become a father at all, but, rather reluctantly, had allowed himself to be persuaded by his wife. For Elizabeth it was unthinkable that she should not become a mother and bring up a family. This was what she had had in mind for herself for as long as she could remember. Besides, she thought, her husband's attitude was bound to change. But it did not. The arrival of Roderick and then Mark hardly triggered off any change in him at all. And just to drive home this point, he would often refer to his young sons as 'Elizabeth's children'. It might have been said tongue in cheek, or, typical of Nicholas, to be provocative and cause a stir. But in reality he was not joking at all. On the contrary, this little quip lay at the very heart of his outlook, which was that since it had been Elizabeth who had been so eager to have children in the first place, she could now assume the bulk of the responsibility for their upbringing.

To their father, then, Roderick and Mark were rather in the way; a couple of also-rans who under no circumstances were to be permitted to prevent him from pursuing his own interests. The origin of this attitude is not difficult to detect. For was this not precisely the same view as Nicholas's own parents had adopted towards him as a young boy? Had he not been regarded as something of a nuisance himself? Ignored and shunned as a child, as an adult he knew of no other pattern of parenting on which to base his own approach to fatherhood.

There might well have been nothing problematic about history repeating itself in this way if Elizabeth had been prepared to devote herself to her sons. Yet Nicholas was not at all happy that she should do so. Rather he insisted on reserving and receiving the lion's share of his wife's attention and affection for himself. In this respect he could not but compete with his sons. As for Elizabeth, she showed insufficient strength of character to strike a satisfactory balance between being a mother on the one hand and a wife on the other. For there was never any doubt as to which way the scales of her affection would tip: inexorably they would come down on her husband's side. The boys would simply have to learn to make do and be grateful for what affection might happen to come their way.

'It's not often that you can say such a thing in a marriage,' Maureen Ellam explains, 'but Elizabeth loved her husband much more than her own sons.' If this was indeed the case, then appearances must have been deceptive. For both Roderick and Mark hardly seemed to be a picture of abuse or neglect. As they grew older few things were denied them. Their parents purchased one set of expensive equipment after another: sports gear, sailing dinghies, all the paraphernalia of scuba diving, and a good deal more besides. Although they were left with nannies when too small to

19

ski themselves, it was not too long before the boys were being flown to the Swiss Alps and the snow. Indeed they were constantly encouraged to pursue sporting and outdoor activities of all kinds, including water-skiing and riding. From the outside, here were all the trappings of a life of luxury and indulgence. And if this existence constituted a picture of denial and depriva-tion, why were Roderick and Mark so often envied by their friends?

'Actually I rather felt sorry for those two boys in a way,' Angela Barnes affirms:

It's true that they had all of these things – and a thoroughly good education too. And I've no doubt that Elizabeth was fond of Roderick and Mark in her own way. But she was always far more attached to Nicholas than to the boys. It is also true that they had everything which money could buy in terms of sporting gear and so on. But they were short of something else not available in smart sports shops, and that was love.

But what was the source of all this money, which seemed to flow so freely during those years? For here was a lifestyle wholly disproportionate to the expecta-tions of two junior-schoolteachers, one of whom worked entirely at his own convenience and the other hardly at all. The answer lay in the past. Both Elizabeth and Nicholas came from monied families and had inherited considerable sums from their parents, Eliza-beth receiving a substantial income from her father's company in Scotland. In fact it was capital she had received from the sale of one of her father's businesses, together with a separate gift from him before his death, which had paid for the purchase of Martello Cottage in the parish of St Brelade. That start had helped the young couple enormously.

At one stage during the late 1960s the Newalls had between them no less than a quarter of a million pounds in shares in the model-car manufacturers De Lesney. When the value of these shares suddenly plummeted, Elizabeth rushed to her stockbroker and instructed him to sell at once, convinced that they would continue to decline. It was the first of many major miscalculations which would cost the couple dearly, and in fact it was this disastrous sale which eventually obliged them to move from Martello Cottage to Crow's Nest. Only when they were settled in their new hilltop home at Grève de Lecq did the shares begin to regain value, by which time the damage had been done.

Despite their rather extravagant lifestyle, the Newalls were in many respects rather naïve when it came to money. Invariably it was Elizabeth who made the key decisions, and more often than not they were the wrong ones. She had once allowed herself to be cheated out of £15,000 by signing up and supplying funds for land in Mexico which, on closer inspection, turned out not to exist at all. And years later she managed to lose £60,000 in one year on shares alone. She had a habit of plumping for the most unusual shares, sometimes against all advice, and very often paid heavily for having done so.

Nan Clark explains:

Elizabeth and Nick were academics really. They were incompetent in many ways, especially with money. They just didn't seem to live and struggle in the real world like everybody else. Elizabeth was always looking for money. She always gave the impression of being hard up. But everything is relative, is it not? Because then, out of the blue, Nick would suddenly present her with a luxury item like a diamond-and-sapphire necklace. To me it just didn't seem to make sense. Not that she spent that much money on herself. But with Nick not earning all that much by way of teaching, their running expenses were far too high. You might say that they led the life of the rich, albeit in a frugal manner.

But how much money makes one rich? Whatever the answer to that question, the Newalls were not within the ranks of the super-rich. And they were most certainly not wealthy by the very special standards of Jersey, where several hundred multimillionaires are comfortably ensconced, lured there not just by its undoubted natural charm but also by its exceptionally attractive fiscal regime. Despite their constantly fluctuating fortunes, and Elizabeth's ample supply of tales of woe, the Newalls were comfortably off, but nothing more remarkable than that. A tremendous snob, Nicholas could boast that he was a Lloyds 'name', a privilege he was able to enjoy by virtue of having disposable assets of at least £100,000. He was happy to be associated with that great British institution, established back in the seventeenth century when underwriters and merchants used to gather informally at Edward Lloyd's coffee house in Tower Street. Indeed so satisfied was Nicholas with his syndicate that in the mid-1980s he had been thinking of significantly increasing his investments – at precisely the time when warning bells were beginning to sound for some names.

Such were the assets, then, that provided the bulk of the Newalls' income. They also had a habit of spreading their resources around the globe, opening bank accounts in London, Scotland, Spain, Switzerland and Andorra. They even had one in Japanese yen, just in case that currency should suddenly start to soar. But if all this speculative activity made them appear to be involved in the very highest of high finance, they were not. For every now and then something would go wrong with their investments and it would be back to the classroom for Nicholas. How many other Lloyds names have ever been obliged to teach history to small children in order to make ends meet?

When the Newalls had money, however, they needed no lessons in spending it. Arriving in London for a shopping spree, Elizabeth would make a beeline for Harrods and splash out on seven pairs of shoes. Maureen Ellam puts it rather succinctly:

They were educated people. Even though they

were good spenders they were very unpretentious with it, and they certainly didn't flash it around. Yes, they did like the good things in life, but they were also quite bohemian in many ways. They could also manage without. Basically they just didn't give a damn as to what anybody else thought.

And then they would come back down to earth again with a bump. Suddenly the money would dry up, usually through financial incompetence on Elizabeth's part. Then the couple would simply make do without it, confident that, as in the past, their fortunes would swing back in their favour before too long. But while waiting for that moment to arrive, they would often call on friends to act as witnesses to the signing of various life-assurance policies when hard cash had become an urgent necessity.

It was this need to raise capital that led the Newalls to meet the Ellams. Unable to produce the finance for the renovation and repair work necessary to Crow's Nest, Elizabeth and Nicholas decided to sell up and move to a much more modest home. It was during the sale and conveyance of their property at Grève de Lecq that the Newalls and the Ellams became friends. Besides, from the early 1980s Elizabeth and Nicholas had been spending a lot less time on Jersey, having discovered the delights of Spain's Costa Blanca.

There seemed to be no logical pattern to the Newalls' spending. Or if there was it was extremely difficult to detect. For just as Elizabeth had been pleading poverty to anyone prepared to lend an ear, she would suddenly emerge again, cheque-book in hand, ready for another spending spree. While continuing to insist that they were going through a particularly difficult patch financially, they nonetheless invested over £12,000 on a personal computer system, with an impressive range of gadgets and extras.

To those friends who witnessed such apparently spontaneous extravagance, it was baffling behaviour indeed. Nor did Elizabeth feel obliged to come up with a plausible explanation. 'Oh, we managed to scrape it together,' she would announce, keeping the details vague. 'The thing is that it's going to keep Nick happy.'

Indeed keeping her husband happy was Elizabeth Newall's main preoccupation in life. And Spain seemed to make him happiest of all. The couple had purchased a villa in the small town of Javea, almost exactly halfway between Valencia and Alicante. Although they had spent a considerable amount of money on it, installing a small swimming pool and, at Elizabeth's insistence, fitting a new kitchen every two to three years, it was by no means luxurious, but situated rather on a modest modern estate. There they led a most active social life, mixing with all sorts of expatriates. Among these were their close friends the Matthews, and the Smileys – the husband a highly respected retired army officer – and they would often dine with Edmundo Ros, the band leader from the forties and fifties who used to run the Coconut Grove Club in London's West End.

Although in practical terms their lives changed little

when they were in Spain – it remained a combination of writing and research for Nicholas, and tennis and socializing for Elizabeth – the Newalls both appeared to be considerably more relaxed, and Nicholas especially so. There, sitting in the sunshine, reading the papers, completing the crossword and sipping a drink, he would let slip the rather starchy and pompous front which he had always insisted on presenting to the world – at least for a little while. In Javea, among new friends, he also found a new and apparently appreciative audience for his repertoire of jokes, which he would deliver with great panache, and as the weeks and months passed, he unwound completely. When some friends, a little the worse for drink, took it upon themselves to undress their host and then launch him naked into his own swimming pool, it did not even cross his mind to complain. In fact when his head popped up above the surface a few moments later, his was the broadest smile of all. It was all a far cry from the stern schoolmaster stalking the corridors of the smart prep schools of Jersey.

Regularly entertaining on their thirty-foot Jersey-registered yacht, *Chanson de Lecq*, the Newalls, already in semi-retirement, were looking forward to many more years in the sun. The boys had completed their schooling. Crow's Nest had been sold. Now they could devote all their energy to precisely what they had had in mind when setting off for the West Indies twenty years earlier: the pursuit of pleasure.

As 1986 drew to a close, the Newalls threw a huge Christmas party for all of their friends in Spain. There were almost eighty guests for lunch, and no expense was spared, the party being fully catered so that Elizabeth could join in the festivities. Spanish champagne flowed freely – alcohol was even more readily available than in Jersey and accordingly consumed in even greater quantities – crackers were pulled, riddles were read and colourful paper hats were donned by all. The Newalls had spent the greater part of the year in Spain, and it had been a thoroughly good one. The new year was full of promise too, for Nicholas and Elizabeth's plans to visit London, Scotland, Sark and Jersey were already at an advanced stage. It seemed as if the sun was shining brightly on the couple.

2

Jack the Lad

The promotional literature said it all: the British Army was looking for potential officers who showed imagination, personality and a zest for life. 'People who are prepared to have a go at anything,' a glossy brochure added challengingly. Roderick Innes Nelson Newall knew that he fitted the bill exactly, and sailed through every stage of the selection procedure. Electing for a short service commission in the Light Division, he graduated from the Military Academy at Sandhurst, rose to the rank of Lieutenant and served as a platoon commander in the Royal Green Jackets, a regiment steeped in battle honours and famed for its bugles, green berets and fast march.

Fit, healthy and handsome, with a wonderful head of sandy-blond hair, Roderick exuded charm and confidence. By the spring of 1987 the dashing young officer was being introduced to Princess Alexandra at a ceremony at Horseguards Parade in London as an extremely promising new recruit. The message from his commanding officers could hardly have been more clear: if Roderick applied himself properly, there was no reason at all why he should not go on to enjoy a glittering military career.

But Roderick soon discovered that Army life was not always as glamorous as the Ministry of Defence brochures depicted it. While carrying out his duties diligently enough, he became bored with the training of recruits at the Regimental Depot division at Winchester and began to wonder whether or not he was really suited for the Army after all. His selection for the Green Jackets' winter expedition to St Moritz, Switzerland, for the annual 'Swift and Bold' Regimental Handicap, prompted him to put aside such doubts, however, at least momentarily, and boosted his morale accordingly. An accomplished sportsman, Roderick completed the famous Cresta Run in 50.74 seconds, a more than respectable showing, and was soon boasting to friends and acquaintances that he had also managed to complete the Run not on a toboggan but on nothing more elaborate than a tea tray. Despite his daredevil streak, Roderick managed to inspire great loyalty in both the men under his command and his fellow officers, earning his colours with them on a series of tours of duty in Germany.

Yet overseas tours of duty were insufficient to retain the interest of Roderick Newall, who still craved further excitement. Perhaps, he announced to family and

friends, he would apply to join the Metropolitan Police
with a view to working his way into their crack anti-
terrorist squad. Then, surely, the adrenalin would flow
both frequently and fast. Other officers from the Royal
Green Jackets had pursued such a path without regret-
ting it, so why not him? But then Roderick appeared to
hesitate. For suddenly, in the late summer of 1987, he
was informed that there was the very strong possibility
of his being offered promotion. He would be based in
Canada, training soldiers in a programme rather similar
to the Outward Bound scheme in which he had already
acquired valuable experience before joining the Army.
It seemed an ideal opportunity. Word had it that, given
Roderick's penchant for sports and physical activity, it
was only a matter of weeks before his promotion would
be formally approved and announced. His faltering
spirits revived once more.

From his earliest days Roderick had been blessed with
good looks. When he arrived at St Michael's at the age
of four, Irene Stevenson was there to welcome him into
Jersey's smartest pre-prep school. With his cheeky,
outgoing personality, he was a most appealing child,
endearing himself not just to his first teacher but to
every member of staff. He was beautiful to look at,
with a temperament to match. It was no particular
hardship, therefore, for Nan Clark, Elizabeth's older
sister, to look after Roderick, and indeed both of the
boys. They would make their way either to Scotland or
Southend, often travelling unaccompanied, in order to
join their aunt during the school holidays. Sometimes,

31

though, she would herself fly out to Jersey in order to take care of her nephews, invariably assisted by the Newalls' nanny, while Elizabeth and Nicholas were away on holiday.

On the face of it, it seems reasonable to assume that since both son and father were present at St Michael's at the same time – one as pupil, the other as the school's history teacher – there might have been an additional bond between the two. Yet this was far from the case, and on one occasion Newall senior failed to recognize his own son, mistakenly filming another boy's winning sports-day performance. He made light of his gaffe, offering the footage to the parents of the boy concerned. For young Roderick, although he was not at that time able to articulate his disappointment, it was no laughing matter but part of a much broader pattern of behaviour which he was reluctantly coming to accept as the norm.

It was the same story when Roderick moved on at the age of eight to become a boarder at Lockers Park preparatory school on the mainland of Britain. For there both parents were noticeable only by their absence, and indeed rarely visited either of their sons, preferring to wait for their return during the school holidays. It was fortunate for Roderick and Mark that both Nan Clark and their parents' close friend Angela Barnes, whose own son attended the same school, made the effort to journey there in order to take the boys out from time to time, usually at weekends. For Elizabeth and Nicholas Newall good schooling was paramount, and they were always at pains to emphasize its importance. However, in propounding this theory with such vigour and enthusiasm they somehow came to confuse two quite separate roles, convincing themselves that good schooling and good parenting were one and the same.

'I would criticize my sister on just one count,' Nan Clark admits:

> She made the boys very competitive of one another. That's why, I think, they began to not get on as they grew older. Elizabeth was very competitive herself – that's how she had come to do so well at sports – so in a sense it was only natural that she should instil this in the boys. As for Nick, well, he was very critical of the boys in all that they did. It seemed to me as if they could do nothing right. He had such high standards for them. And I think that they both eventually came to tire of that. He was adamant that they should go on to the very best public school in England. Nothing less would do.

And Nicholas Newall harboured not the slightest doubt that Radley College, near Abingdon in Oxfordshire, was that school. Founded in 1847 to provide a public-school education based on the principles of the Church of England, it lies in a beautiful 800-acre park part of which was laid out by 'Capability' Brown, the celebrated landscape gardener and architect. Radley's academic standards have always been exceptionally high, with many boys going on to Oxford or Cambridge. It was hardly surprising, therefore, that when

33

both Roderick and Mark were admitted to the prestigious establishment their parents were overjoyed. All of the pushing and preparation had apparently paid off, for by gaining places at such a distinguished school had not each son in effect been handed a passport to Oxbridge and the professions?

Arriving at Radley, Roderick found himself obliged to learn a new and specialist vocabulary, much of it intelligible only to fellow Radleians. For each of the school's six hundred boys belonged to one of eight houses, or 'Socials', and became accountable to a Social Tutor whose prime responsibility was the smooth running of his particular patch. Roderick found himself in D Social under the watchful eye of Tony Hudson. Radley was a world steeped in its own traditions, such as 'leave-away' and 'privilege weekends', and 'wet-bobs' or 'dry-bobs' in the area of sport. But it was no less enjoyable for that, and Roderick soon struck up a close friendship with another pupil, Charlie Shaw, the son of the hard-living Irish actor the late Robert Shaw.

In fact Roderick soon proved himself to be a most generous schoolfriend, often helping out less able classmates at chemistry and sometimes taking it upon himself to carry out their 'prep'. So obliging was he that on one occasion the chemistry master became highly suspicious when a number of boys presented results which were so strikingly similar that even with the best will in the world they could not be attributed to coincidence. The hand of Roderick Newall was not difficult to detect and he was punished accordingly, together with his co-conspirators. Not that any of them complained, for it was all part of the fun and excitement at Radley. As for the chemistry master, he could at least console himself with the fact that the work had been both accurate and concise. Roderick soon came to fit the mould of the typical Radleian, full of bravado, bubbling with public-school banter and repartee, cocky with his own sex while remaining highly uncomfortable with women – an affliction from which he would in due course make a rapid recovery indeed.

'The Radleians I remember had no subtlety when it came to girls,' a female contemporary recalls, 'they would go charging off to balls in a pack, getting ridiculously drunk and returning with tall tales for each other – all heard with a willing suspension of disbelief.'

Rod, as he was known to his friends, soon developed a reputation as the liveliest of live wires, part and parcel of Radley's lunatic fringe. Excitement and adventure became his *raison d'être*. And his eccentricities were most apparent when he was living in the Mansion, one of the school's several buildings of architectural distinction. There he would dance around on the edge of the roof, suspending himself precariously from its ledge, and flirting with danger whenever and wherever the opportunity presented itself. It was thus fortunate, not least for his own safety, that by far the greater part of Roderick's considerable energy came to be channelled into sport. The school's sports provision was excellent, for its well-equipped indoor complex included five squash courts, a heated swimming pool, a multi-purpose sports hall, and sub-aqua activities, sailing and windsurfing were also available. And with the

River Thames only a stone's throw away, many boys took up rowing, Roderick soon proving to be one of the best oarsmen. Of average height but above average strength, he excelled in all sports, his versatility and achievements as an all-rounder undoubtedly contributing to his growing popularity.

Oxford was only five miles away, and Roderick would often make his way into town. One could never be sure what mischief he might get up to, but one thing was certain: he was not there to view that city's many fine spires. Sometimes it would be to shop, true enough, but more often than not it was to top up his supply of drugs, the most recent source of Radley-based stimulation for Roderick, and always readily available in the city centre. After a while he became quite blasé about his drug-taking, although naturally not with his schoolmasters, as he knew that he risked expulsion should he be caught red-handed. In all probability the high stakes made the forbidden fruit all the more seductive, and sometimes Roderick would frankly admit its appeal. 'Much better for you, this, you know,' he would insist, drawing on a joint, 'than all of that stuff,' pointing either to cigarettes or alcohol.

Occasionally, back in Jersey for the school holidays, Roderick and Mark would do some gardening for Angela Barnes. In Roderick's case it was certainly not for the love of nature or fresh air, but simply to boost his funds. The Newalls' friend remembers:

I didn't need the boys here to garden. It was just to help them out. Because Nick always told them to work for their money: not that he was averse to taking the odd hand out himself, mind you. I didn't really want Roderick to do the gardening, to be honest, but I allowed him to. Actually he did b— all. While his brother would sit down and sip water, Roderick would always ask for beer. As the years went by you could see that he actually led a much fuller life than Mark. He wasn't such a thinker, not nearly as deep as his brother. In fact I always used to feel that Roderick had a most devious look. He would hardly ever look straight at you. There was definitely something about him, although I could never quite put my finger on it. Tricky eyes, I always used to say.

Relations between Roderick and Nicholas Newall might well have been strained, but the former was certainly very fond of his father's twin brother, Stephen. Roderick would often spend holidays in Scotland together with his uncle and aunt, staying at the family home, an imposing castellated granite edifice near Rhu. During term time he would look forward to meeting up with relatives and in particular his cousin Amanda, to whom he was very close. Most exciting of all though was the prospect of spending time on his uncle's private island of Shuna, off the west coast. Here was something to boast about to the boys at school. How many other Radleians held such an impressive trump card?

Despite the first-class academic record of Radley College, neither of the Newall boys won a place at university. Not that any teacher doubted the ability or intelligence of the brothers; it was simply that they proved not to be cast in the academic mould. Roderick in particular was destined to be a man of action, not words. The prospect of his sons bypassing further education altogether came as an enormous disappointment to Nicholas Newall. He had always been keen to endorse and cite Radley's motto, borrowed from Thoreau: 'Not failure, but low aim, is crime.' Could Roderick not be indicted on precisely that count, he wondered, of having set his sights too low? At a stroke, all his hopes and expectations for his sons were dashed. He had steadfastly maintained that the correct life for a gentleman was university, followed by entry into one of the professions – engineering, medicine or law. A graduate himself, he had assumed that the day would come when he would sit and applaud his sons at their degree ceremony. It is easy to imagine his sense of failure, then, when Roderick began to mention the possibility of pursuing a military career. Yet for the young school-leaver it seemed an eminently sensible thing to do. He had thrived in Radley's Combined Cadet Force. Was there any logical reason, he would retort, why his passion for excitement, sport and adventure should not be allowed to develop on a sound professional basis, within the disciplined framework of the Army? In the event a compromise was reached. Roderick would go abroad for a year in order to gain experience and broaden his horizons, a period which would at the same time afford him an opportunity to reflect on his future. No hasty decisions would be made.

When he returned from a year in Australia, Roderick's mind was made up. He was going to apply for a short service commission after all. But before doing so he would work for a while with John Ridgeway, a mountaineer and instructor of international repute. Based at Ridgeway's Outward Bound school in the west of Scotland, it was a placement which Elizabeth Newall had helped to secure. Always happiest when out in the open, Roderick found the work both challenging and stimulating. But it was also there, in the fresh air of Scotland, that he allowed his temper to get the better of him. He and his mother were alike not just in looks and their flair for sport, but temperamentally too. For Elizabeth's elder son had undoubtedly inherited her renowned volatility.

Throughout his childhood and adolescence Roderick had fought a losing battle to control his fierce and fiery outbursts. Over the years every member of the Newall family had witnessed similar scenes unfold on numerous occasions. They had all come to recognize the warning signs rather well – and woe betide whoever happened to be present should young Roderick not get his way. Erupting within the family, however, was one thing; erupting in public, quite another. John Ridgeway's regulations were well known to all members of staff; nor did they discriminate against Roderick in any way. It was simply that liaisons between the sexes were strictly forbidden. But when a most attractive girl started work at the school Roderick chose to ignore completely this particular prohibition. The head of the mountaineering school did not appreciate this flagrant breach of the rules. But instead of accepting a reprimand from Ridgeway, Roderick decided to lash out, first with his tongue and then with his fists, and a fight soon broke out between the two men. Having left the camp in a hurry, Roderick beat a hasty retreat to London, where he stayed with his Aunt Nan, his girlfriend with him, eager to accompany her hot-headed lover.

As suddenly as Roderick's temper would flare, so too would it subside. And when he was behaving rationally, there was no doubt that he could be very charming. By the age of nineteen he found himself on the edge of high society, introduced to a crowd of jet-setting friends in London by a Radley soul mate. Conspicuous consumption was their motto. A number of Roderick's contemporaries were already firmly established as part of the 'beagle and Bollinger set', and some were the owners of private planes despite still being in their teens. Although he had enjoyed more than a taste of high living when in Jersey, and had observed at close quarters how the rich and pampered lived, he was enormously excited to have discovered and now be part of an in crowd himself.

Beautifully spoken, wild, daring and seductive, Roderick was attractive to women and enjoyed all the advantages which his striking good looks conferred on him, bedding one female admirer after another. Naturally image was all important – the clothes and the car both had to be right – and that meant slick, fast and flashy. He bought himself an MGB GT and wrote it off within a fortnight. Not that that distressed him unduly; he knew it would be dealt with by his insurers. It was typical of Roderick's approach: easy come, easy go. Rather like his parents, in fact, he was out to lead the good life. Or, as Maureen Ellam's husband, David, used to put it, Roderick's personality was not at all difficult to sum up: Jack the Lad.

When Elizabeth Newall heard of Roderick's fight with John Ridgeway she was horrified and ashamed. But she was hardly surprised, for over the years she had witnessed dozens of such outbursts by her son. Her concern was much more immediate and pragmatic: that should the Army hear of this incident, then Roderick's chances of ever being accepted by the Royal Military Academy would become slender indeed. She wondered what she could do to help, and then she remembered that her friends in Spain, the Smileys, had very good connections within military circles and she set about using these contacts to her advantage. Elizabeth had never shared Nicholas's rather haughty attitude towards their son's desire to pursue a military career. Therefore when Roderick finally walked through the main entrance at Sandhurst, to begin his officer training, she breathed an enormous sigh of relief. Now at last, she felt, her elder son would receive a proper dose of discipline, and not before time.

Or would he? For while Roderick did indeed come to terms with the rigours of the parade ground, and soon mastered the art of firing a rifle and other small arms with great precision, his underlying character did not change at all. Within a few weeks he was up to old tricks, notably with drugs. Aware that one of the men in his own platoon was heavily dependent on illegal substances, Roderick soon entered into a most unconventional relationship with him: the Royal Green Jackets officer doubled as his subordinate's supplier. It was all a far cry from the disciplined environment for which Elizabeth Newall had hoped for so long.

Although they often got on well together, being alike in many ways, Roderick and Elizabeth frequently clashed. And one particular day they did so most fiercely. On leave from Germany, Roderick had returned to Jersey. Not for the first time, he brought up the subject of money, and asked his mother for additional funds, as he was in some difficulty meeting his mess bills. Although in the past she had viewed such requests sympathetically, sometimes even going against her husband's rulings on these matters, this time she decided not to reach for her cheque-book. Standing in the kitchen in front of her stove, she pointed out to her son that since he was now in receipt of his own pay as a soldier, he really ought to be able to fend for himself. After all, every other officer managed to do so.

It was not at all what Roderick had been expecting to hear. Clenching his fists in a fit of rage, he rushed over to his mother and punched her about the top of the back and neck, making her cry out in pain. Sitting at his word processor in another part of the house, Nicholas Newall heard the commotion coming from the kitchen and ran as fast as he could to find out what was happening to his wife. Without waiting for any explanation, he told Elizabeth to leave the room, saying that he would sort out his son himself. It was not necessary to launch a protracted inquiry. Roderick had simply lost control yet again.

'One Sunday morning at eleven o'clock,' Angela Barnes recalls:

Elizabeth suddenly turned up. I was always pleased to see my friend, but on this occasion she was in a most dreadful state. She said, 'Roderick has just attacked me,' and burst into tears. She told me how he had asked for some money but that she had turned him down. Poor Elizabeth was very uncomfortable, and I told her that I would arrange for a friend of mine to come round and massage her back and neck outside on my terrace. I thought that might help to relieve the tension and stop any bruising from flaring up. She knew that she wouldn't be able to play tennis for ages and was worried what she would say to other people. She was like a child in a way, just inconsolable. By the time Nick came round at seven in the evening, she had got through one whole litre of whisky on her own. Nick said that all was well, and gave the impression that Roderick would never dare do such a thing again.

The young lieutenant returned to Germany to rejoin his platoon. He could come up with no compelling reason for his behaviour, other than that a feeling had surged up from within, so powerful that it had made

43

him momentarily take leave of his senses. Waiting for him was a message which his superiors knew he would not like at all: the promotion which had seemed to be so certain, and which was to have taken him to Canada, was not going to be offered after all. In one respect this helped, for now his mind was made up: he would leave the Army at the first available opportunity. What was the correct procedure, he wondered, for applying to the Metropolitan Police? Having put to the back of his mind his assault on his mother, he had the temerity to turn to her again, renewing his plea for financial assistance. Would she consider helping him buy himself out of the Army?

'Most certainly not,' Elizabeth retorted on receiving the request. 'You've got to see your service through. It will do you good. You need the discipline.'

By the summer of 1987 Nan Clark noticed that her nephews appeared to be developing a friendship which had been absent in earlier years. The brothers had hitherto maintained little contact with one another, each going his own way after leaving Radley. But Mark suddenly became a regular visitor to Roderick's barracks at Winchester. Their aunt was delighted, for the era of sibling rivalry which had lasted so long had apparently come to an end:

I was rather relieved, I must admit. Because I thought that all of their squabbling was over. One day I saw that Roderick was wearing a rather nice designer sweatshirt and I commented on it. 'Oh yes, Mark gave it to me,' Roderick said with some pride. I was pleased about that because I used to find their earlier competing for attention and attempts to out-do one another quite trying. It was refreshing to see them getting along so nicely.

Yet there must have been something troubling Nan Clark, if only unconsciously, because during the night of Saturday 10 October 1987 she had a most vivid nightmare. It was so powerful that she jotted down its contents at the time:

We were driving through a forest while it was raining. As we moved forwards we caught up with another vehicle. We soon recognized the shape of a hearse. Then I saw Nicholas sitting on the back. He was smiling and there were two postilions either side of him. These postilions then became like gargoyles and I shouted out to Nicholas. 'What are you doing there?' I called. 'And where is Elizabeth?' At that moment the hearse stopped. Elizabeth got out with her back towards me. But then she turned to her left to look at me. She had a look of resignation on her face. She said: 'I told you it would happen. I told you that he meant it when he said he would kill me.' There was a red brick building to her right, with long, low steps. I began to shout out at the top of my voice: 'Nicholas, Nicholas.'

It was at that point that Nan Clark's husband, Alister, woke up his wife. 'Don't worry,' he said soothingly, 'it's just a dream.'

3

'Serious Crime in Jersey
Is Very Rare'

'I came to Jersey in 1964,' Graham Nimmo explains.

I had just come out of the merchant navy and a lot
of my friends were already over here on the island.
It was only meant to be for a fortnight's holiday.
But I decided to stay. I got myself a job driving a
lorry for Le Riches, the supermarket chain. To
begin with I must say that I found the local people
really difficult to get to know. I used to go into this
pub about three times a week. You could get fairly
merry in those days on about ten bob; that was
including a packet of fags and leaving you a fair
amount of small change too. It was only after
about three or four months though that the licensee bothered to prick up his ears and talk to me. I
had been chatting about the Hanratty murder

case. My father was then the head of the CID in Manchester. I had previously tried to join the Manchester police force, because it had always been my ambition to follow in his footsteps. But the old man had torn up my application form. He didn't want me in the same force as him. As I got to know the licensee I told him that I was looking for a decent job. He happened to know a recruiting inspector in the States of Jersey police force. I think that my father's position must have helped to get me in because it's not often that they take on an outsider like me. They sent me off to Coventry to train. After that I began as a young PC on the beat. I was very happy indeed.

As PC Graham Nimmo began walking his beat around the backstreets of St Helier, he could find little of the high drama which, in subsequent years, would occupy the minds of the producers of *Bergerac*. Nevertheless the BBC television series is one of the main reasons, according to research carried out by Jersey's department of tourism, why visitors continue to be attracted to the island. Nor could Nimmo's team really be said to resemble the *Bergerac* squad: for in the 1960s the local police force could not even muster a single radio between them, having to rely instead on prearranged two-hourly meetings at strategically selected telephone booths scattered around the town. In fact on Graham Nimmo's first night out on beat number five, he was unable even to find the Albert Street phone box which was meant to double as his rendezvous point, let alone arrest any wrongdoers.

The notion of Jersey as a hive of criminal activity could hardly be further from the truth. One who should know is John Nettles, the leading actor in the successful detective series. 'Despite its television image,' he points out in a bid to dispel the many myths he has helped to create, 'serious crime in Jersey is very rare.'

The island's overall crime rate, however, is on a par with many parts of the United Kingdom. Nevertheless armed robbery hardly ever occurs, for where could robbers run to on a strip of land of only nine miles by five? Over half of all crime committed is carried out by itinerant workers employed during the summer months. And that means mostly petty crime like shop-lifting and drinking offences. The States of Jersey police force, based at its Rouge Bouillon headquarters in the heart of St Helier, prefers to promote a much warmer and more homely image, far removed from intrigue and suspense. A plaque placed prominently at the entrance to police HQ spells out that approach: 'The British bobby is renowned throughout the world for a helpful and courteous attitude towards the millions of overseas visitors to Britain. It is in this spirit that the States of Jersey police and the Island's honorary police welcome you to Jersey.'

While there is a Drugs Unit on the island and a Commercial Branch specializing in the investigation of fraud, the Jersey police force still managed to find a good deal of time during 1987 to raise money for a number of deserving causes. 'Operation Goodwill' concentrated on raising funds for a number of charities active on the island. Police officers always appeared eager to give generously of their time when it came to raising money for the unfortunate and underprivileged, nine members of the force successfully completing a sponsored parachute jump which raised over £1300 and was dubbed 'Cop Drop' by the local press. Here was community policing at its best, people pulling together for the good of the community. Indeed a sense of family and belonging still pervades the vast majority of the population, whatever their social status. It is hardly surprising, therefore, that the Chief Officer's report for 1987 managed to find space to dwell on the fate of one of the force's four dogs, Jet, who had been unexpectedly retired after the diagnosis of heart disease. This had distressed his handler, PC Hafey, who had previously put the dog through his paces to the delight of spectators in a series of demonstrations and displays at fêtes and fairs all over the island.

In the spring of 1987 officers were called out to investigate an incident which had all the hallmarks of the problems experienced by Jersey's wealthy socialites. As officers made their way to a home in Bon Air Lane, one of the island's more stylish spots, they found that a Madeiran housekeeper by the name of Fatima Ornelas, outraged and incensed by the terms and conditions of her employment, had deliberately reversed her employer's car into the family's large moon-shaped swimming pool. Mrs Ornelas had been able to effect her escape from the vehicle because the pool's cover had been in place, although the car had started to sink within a few seconds of her hasty exit via the driver's door. As this incident was taking place, telephone calls were being received at the substation at St Brelade. In response to these, Sergeant Terry Mac-Donald and his team of four constables set off to investigate the mystery of a one-and-a-half-ton Friesian cow which had been washed up on the beach not far from the Hotel L'Horizon, having already spent some time floating conspicuously close to the shore.

And then suddenly the police agenda would change again. Manpower now had to be devoted to ensure the smooth running and security of the visit to Jersey by the Duke and Duchess of York. They had been invited as the guests of honour in the 1987 Golden Jubilee celebrations for the island's small but extremely active airport. As Prince Andrew and 'Fergie' were whisked around the island from one event to another, being given the red carpet treatment at all times, most members of the States of Jersey force agreed: when it came to the policing of their patch, there was never a dull moment.

The entire force in Jersey is itself a relatively recent creation, for right up until the middle of the present century no fewer than eleven of the island's twelve parishes policed themselves without any assistance from the 'professional police' at all. Then, if a crime was reported, Jersey's unique system of justice would swing into action. The head of the parish – the Constable – would be alerted. He in turn would contact his honorary policemen, including the Centenier and

51

his Vingteniers. It was policing by part-timers in pullovers. Only after the end of the Second World War did things begin to alter, but the pace of change was leisurely indeed. By 1950 there were still only fifty full-time policemen on the island, with five times that fifty operating as honorary police officers. However arbitrary and amateurish this approach to policing might have been, the system certainly appeared to work well and in the interests of all law-abiding islanders.

'My advance within the police force was painfully slow,' Graham Nimmo recalls.

It was a question of dead men's shoes. Eventually I went to the CID on a three-month secondment. I always wanted to be a detective, like my dad, I suppose. I had a cracking job there. I worked together with a chap named Phil Falle, who later went on to become the chief crime correspondent for our local paper, the *Jersey Evening Post*. Together we arrested twenty-three receivers and two hotel-breakers. That got me recognized, I guess, and I stayed there until 1976, when I became a sergeant and went back into uniform. I loved the work. So it was no hardship at all for me to put in a sixteen-hour day. I used to live for it.

By 1987, however, things were beginning to become considerably less cosy on the island. The Chief Officer, David Parkinson, complained to the President and members of the Defence Committee in his annual report that it had been a particularly difficult and trying year for the force. Three police officers, including a Detective Chief Inspector, had been accused but acquitted of conspiring to pervert the course of justice, so that the full glare of publicity was fixed firmly on Jersey's troubled force. And for the first time in the island's history, it was statistics rather than burglaries which were causing alarm bells to sound, for the total of reported crimes exceeded five thousand. Nor was Martyn Le Brocq a happy man. As Chief Inspector of Crime, he complained that it was difficult to launch any major inquiry without computerized facilities. A manual system was simply not as efficient, he insisted, however competent and eager the trained personnel. But no additional resources had been made available, despite a recommendation to that effect made by Her Majesty's Inspector of Constabulary after his visit to Jersey the previous year. Martyn Le Brocq sought to take comfort from statistics; that the island's rate of crime detection remained well above the UK average, and stood at an impressive forty per cent. But even he was obliged to admit that Jersey's own figures for the successful detection of crime were down compared with previous years. It was all very disappointing. Nor were there that many crumbs of consolation to be picked up from the fact that at least one of the year's more serious crimes had not taken place on Jersey soil, a resident of the island being jailed for four years by Exeter Crown Court on the mainland. Ian Walker had received his custodial sentence after insisting that his wife eat a Mars bar which, he omitted to tell her, he had laced with a lethal quantity of caustic soda.

For David Le Quesne, however, one of the island's up-and-coming young lawyers, 1987 had been anything but a disappointing year. He had recently managed to recruit some new clients, Elizabeth and Nicholas Newall, for his firm of advocates, Vibert & Valpy. And within the small, tightly-knit legal community of Jersey, he gave the impression of a man who was going places, a talented advocate determined to make a name for himself by establishing a large and thriving practice. Like most residents in Jersey, David Le Quesne was worried about the increase in crime on the island. A family man, he wondered if the trend was irreversible. But at the same time he had reason to know better than most that more crime meant more work. He describes his own career thus:

> I originally qualified as a British barrister, becoming a member of the Inner Temple, but I soon realized that I would be better off as a medium fish in a medium pool, rather than as a small fish in an enormous pool. So that meant coming back to Jersey to practise. I have always been fascinated by crime. And in particular I enjoy reading about murder. Unfortunately I've only ever been involved in two capital cases previously. But whether you are reading or pleading, you can't beat a good murder.

On 1 October 1987 Graham Nimmo finally achieved what he had been hoping for for some time: promotion from Sergeant to the rank of Detective Inspector. And a few months earlier he had received a Long Service and Good Conduct medal. For the burly, outgoing forty-six-year-old, Perth-born but Manchester-bred, things were working out very nicely indeed. Finally, it seemed, recognition was coming his way. Now the only person above him was Martyn Le Brocq himself, but as the Chief Inspector was invariably office-bound the newly appointed Detective Inspector had in effect become the most senior operational detective on the island. Any major criminal investigation would henceforth fall within his sphere of responsibility. It was fortunate for Graham Nimmo, therefore, that he enjoyed a good working relationshp with his right-hand man, Sergeant Jimmy Adamson, an officer with a reputation for his gritty determination.

Despite the undoubted pressures of their work, many of the more senior members of the States of Jersey police enjoy a rather attractive lifestyle. A number of officers have not been slow to take advantage of a combination of generous remuneration and Jersey's geographical position, buying holiday homes in nearby Normandy and Brittany. And although courses constitute part of the ongoing process of their training, most officers report that renewed contact with the mainland can both refresh and revitalize. Certainly this was the experience of Inspector Paul Marks, who attended a Special Branch course at New Scotland Yard during 1987, and Detective Inspector Martin Fitzgerald, who likewise left the island briefly to participate in a television and radio skills programme organized by the

Police Staff College at Bramshill. All in all, it was not a bad life. Certainly *Bergerac* never seemed to have it so good. As Graham Nimmo admits:

I was really pleased with that promotion to Detective Inspector, because that had always been my ambition. It gave me the opportunity to be outdoors, not desk-bound, which I have always preferred. For many years prior to that though I had become fascinated and intrigued by dead bodies and murder – any suspicious death in fact. I always insisted upon going along to the mortuary and would work closely with the pathologist. I was not satisfied until I had seen where the bullet had gone in and where it had come out. If you had a body lying there I wanted to know all about it. The only thing which would really get to me and upset me was the death of a child or baby. Other than that I somehow seemed to be able to cut off from the horror of it all. In fact I once disgusted everybody by eating my sandwiches at the same time as a post-mortem was being carried out. I was always keen to increase my knowledge of forensic medicine and would do my best to ensure that I could attend additional courses wherever possible; I couldn't absorb the information quickly enough. And I have to say that by the time of my promotion I had also established a pretty good track record: I had never once lost a murder case which I had been responsible for bringing to court. So you can imagine that now that I was going to be part of the team responsible for most serious crime committed on the island, it felt really good to be back working within the CID.

Nevertheless, as Detective Inspector Nimmo sat behind his desk at police headquarters at Rouge Bouillon, sporting his new 'pips', there seemed little to whet the appetite of someone with his particular interest in criminality. The last public execution in Jersey had been back in 1875. The death penalty had likewise been erased from the statute books. And while the police report for 1987 recorded that there had been no fewer than 2242 theft-related offences reported during the year, constituting some forty per cent of the island's crime, the column which really interested Graham Nimmo lay elsewhere in that document. It was the data that came under the general heading of 'offences against the person' but was categorized more precisely as 'murder and manslaughter'. Here was the material which had consistently caught Nimmo's eye first. But in the space allocated to these statistics no entry had been made at all. Not that there was any mystery surrounding this omission: it was simply that there had apparently been no such grisly crimes to record. All the same, as the Detective Inspector continued to cast a professional eye up and down the document he could not help wondering when the next official murder inquiry might come his way.

4

Yuppy

Everybody agreed: he had got on exceptionally well; and in such a short space of time too. Scarcely out of school, Mark Newall was already demonstrating a capacity to make money which had endeared him to his employers while making him the envy of his friends. Every inch the yuppy, he boasted a fancy sports car and a bank balance with a rate of acceleration to match. At nineteen he had his own table at one of Jersey's smartest restaurants, Victoria's, part of the Grand Hotel on the Esplanade in St Helier. It was an arrangement which fitted in with his requirements very well. For not only was the food excellent, but the premises were within easy walking distance of his office at the firm of brokers Sheppards, one of the thousands of financial institutions seeking to take advantage of Jersey's very attractive fiscal regime. But the sight of the young financier sitting alone, eating an evening meal, hardly caused heads to turn. And even for those with whom he had had some personal contact in the past, considerably more than a single sighting of solitary dining had been required before the truth had begun to dawn. But once it did it was as clear as could be: no matter how deft a hand Mark Newall might be when it came to wheeling and dealing in Euro-bonds, it would have been difficult to find a lonelier and more isolated figure on the island of Jersey.

If only those who might momentarily have felt sorry for Mark had known that what they were witnessing was merely part of a much broader solitude. Had they witnessed the scene on Christmas morning in 1986, for example, their hearts would surely have reached out to him even more. For while brother Roderick was celebrating with fellow officers in the Royal Green Jackets and as their parents were throwing a lavish party for numerous friends and acquaintances at their villa in Spain, Mark had awoken to a cold and empty house, bare of decorations and similarly devoid of any seasonal spirit. In a way, having been told where his present was made matters even worse. The shirt had been wrapped several months earlier and put away in a bottom drawer in another part of the house. It was Mark's responsibility, now that the morning of 25 December had arrived, to unwrap his parents' offering. That task completed, Mark's Christmas festivities were over – hardly a day to remember. Another time, when he had journeyed to his parents' villa in Javea

with a view to escaping from the pressures of work
and basking for a few days in the sun, he had found
himself holidaying there alone. But then this had
been the pattern almost from the outset: Mark's
parents had hardly ever been there for him at all.
Corinne Symonds recalls:

> My son Nicholas asked me if I could have Mark
> over on that Christmas day, but I had just been
> diagnosed as having cancer – with a major
> operation booked in for shortly after the new
> year. I said that I just couldn't do as he asked –
> that it was too much for me. Nicholas was
> furious, saying that I had no right to call myself a
> Christian and that I ought to be ashamed. After
> a day or so I relented and thought that perhaps
> one more would not make much difference after
> all. But by that time another family had offered
> to take him in.

Mark and Nicholas Symonds had struck up a friendship when working together at Barclaytrust in St
Helier during the early 1980s. Another point of
contact was that several years earlier Mark's father
had been Nicholas's teacher for a while, during his
time at St Michael's school. It was a typical Jersey
connection, on an island where everyone seemed to
know everyone. As islanders often joke among themselves: 'It isn't who you know or what you know; it's
what you know about who you know.'

The two young men found that they had much in

common: an interest in rugby, a dry, public-school sense of humour and an interest in good cars and good health. They would often jog together along Jersey's longest single stretch of tarmac, La Grande Route des Mielles, now more popularly known as Five Mile Road, at St Ouen's, chatting away animatedly all the time, Nicholas's dog happy to be given an unusually long run. Ever since injuring his knee at Radley, Mark had been aware of the importance of keeping fit and trim, often going out of his way to put in a few extra hours of weight-training.

'He led a typical bachelor type of life,' Nicholas Symonds explains.

He would get in late from work, hire a couple of videos, buy a Chinese or Indian take-away, that sort of thing. Sometimes I would go round and notice what a mess the house was in, with several days' worth of previous take-aways piled up in great heaps. Mark wouldn't let you feel sorry for him though. He wouldn't ask you for anything. We became pretty close friends, I guess, but he didn't let anyone in at all really. He was desperately introverted and withdrawn, especially with girls. You couldn't help getting the impression that there was something which wasn't quite right, although it was very difficult to put your finger on it. Maybe it was because of the many barriers that he put up – but I couldn't help feeling sorry for him all the same. I just used to think that he had a rather sad existence. That's

why I had been so keen for my mum to ask him
round on that particular Christmas day.

Most islanders do not like to admit it. The fact
remains, however, that although tourism and horti-
culture are enormously important in raising revenue
for the States' Treasury, it is without doubt high
finance which has become the mainstay of Jersey's
economy. So successful has the island been in establishing itself as a major centre of international
finance, that it is now a multimillion-pound industry
generating massive taxes, sufficient to pay for all of
its health and educational requirements, as well as
expenditure of many other kinds. St Helier bristles
with banks of every description, from the Hong Kong
and Shanghai Banking Corporation to the Bank of
Bermuda, with some sixty further banks from dozens
of other countries.

The finance era had been ushered in during the
early 1960s when a usury law restricting interest rates
to five per cent had been abolished. The brainchild of
the late Senator Cyril Le Marquand, it was a deliber-
ate attempt to attract investors, and proved to be
successful beyond his wildest dreams. Merchant
bankers seeking a low-tax base from which to service
clients had not been slow to spot the unique potential
offered by the Channel Islands: close to the City of
London, beyond its jurisdiction and yet with a political system designed to ensure long-term stability.
Kleinwort Benson, Hill Samuel and the Royal Trust
of Canada had been the first to move in, with other

large institutions wasting little time in following suit. The offshore finance business developed so rapidly that Jersey soon became home to billions of pounds' worth of deposits, held by countless financial concerns of every shade and variety, with billions of pounds of additional funds being handled by local trust companies.

It is only when pressed or cross-questioned, however, that its inhabitants will admit that Jersey has come to be so dependent upon the financial services industry. Many islanders regret that the pace of change has been so fast and furious. It all seems a far cry, they lament, from the old, more relaxed and rural way of life. Mark Newall, however, suffered from no such restraints. On the contrary, here was a world which represented opportunity and excitement; one into which, therefore, he moved with great relish and ease. Financially ambitious, he felt confident that he could succeed. He found employment easily enough, his curriculum vitae impressing Barclaytrust, with whom he started work as a trainee administrator in the company trust and administration department. But it soon became clear to him that this was hardly what he had had in mind.

Nevertheless it was there that Mark acquired a number of important basic skills, such as dealing with simple business correspondence, administering trusts and handling minor investments. Yet he still lacked real power. As he set about executing his various tasks, organizing meetings of shareholders and directors on behalf of the private companies for which he was responsible, he realized that there could be no question of his pursuing a lengthy career within the confines of Barclaytrust. The bank's policy was too slow, too prudent, too cautious by far. Everything other than the most menial of tasks had to be referred upwards to his boss, Michael Blackey, or another more experienced member of the team. There was hardly any scope for initiative or enterprise, let alone risk-taking. Before long he began to ponder his next move.

Pat Stoker, recalling the days when the younger Newall boy worked with him at Barclaytrust, asserts:

> Mark was a very presentable and confident young man during his time with us, and he could most certainly impress a client from his speech and appearance. I felt that he had a certain arrogance about him though, considering that the work which he was carrying out was somehow beneath him. I think that his view was that in order to get on he would have to get out.

And that is precisely what he did. Sheppards (Channel Islands) Limited, by contrast, fitted in with Mark's self-image very well indeed. With offices on the Esplanade, here was a firm specializing in Euro-bonds, a fast-moving, twenty-four-hour market which Mark embraced wholeheartedly. Most satisfying of all was the fact that his new boss, Graham Lovett, ensured that his bright and enthusiastic new employee was allocated sufficient space to be able to perform effectively. Mark did not disappoint him.

The young broker would sometimes arrive at the office at six a.m. and put in a good day's work, only to be the last one to leave that evening. And with the economy soaring during the Thatcherite boom of the mid-1980s, there was seldom any shortage of deals waiting to be done. Just as the New York Stock Market was closing, so Tokyo would be opening. It was an all-consuming world, almost tailor-made for Mark in that it was entirely effective in enabling him to ward off his underlying sense of isolation. With hardly enough time for lunch, loneliness seldom caught him unawares. And, most satisfying of all, a combination of a good salary and even better commissions made for a very lucrative package indeed.

'I am not one to shower compliments on Mark,' says Angela Barnes:

> But when it comes to the handling of money I have to admit that he is something of a financial genius. He was soon dealing with his parents' money, and with spectacular results too. He once doubled £75,000 of Elizabeth and Nicholas's money within a few weeks. They were delighted. I began to wonder whether or not he might be able to do likewise with my own funds. Who wouldn't?

Yet there had been a time, not so long before, when Nicholas Newall had shown considerably less enthusiasm about the prospect of his son handling the family's financial affairs. For quite some time he had steadfastedly refused to allow Mark to become a signatory and thus able to act on his behalf. It was only a combination of his determination to spend an increasing amount of time in Spain and Elizabeth's unshakeable faith in her younger son's abilities that had finally persuaded Nicholas to change his mind.

Ideally positioned to assess the wisdom of his parents' investments, Mark took the view that his father should withdraw from his Lloyds syndicate as soon as possible. He had reason to believe that all was far from well in the international insurance marketing association in London. So adamant was he that his father should no longer be associated with Lloyds that the young broker could not prevent himself from making an impassioned plea to that effect whenever an opportunity presented itself. What Mark failed to appreciate, however, was that his father was extremely proud of being a Lloyds name, an achievement which he was not about to relinquish lightly. On the contrary, he was rather keen to increase his investments there, infuriating his son still further.

'If he had been working in London you would have said he was a typical city whizz-kid,' Nicholas Symonds says of Mark.

You know: work, home and into new car. He had a twin-cam sixteen-valve Toyota and then a Toyota MR2 sports. But he couldn't really be bothered to look after them. So he used to pay me £25 to clean his car for him while he was at work. He was always smart in his appearance. The lifestyle suited the type of job he had. He was

totally involved in his work. That was his existence. No discos or anything. Just working himself
stupid from dawn to dusk.

Unlike Roderick, who liked to smoke and drink, quite
apart from his long-standing involvement with drugs,
Mark had scarcely any interest in alcohol. While Nicholas Symonds and his group of rugby-playing friends
downed huge quantities of beer without any great
effort, Mark would sit quietly sipping a vodka and fruit
juice. And even that was really only to be sociable. For
Mark Newall there were few things less appealing in
life than the prospect of an evening's heavy drinking,
the undeclared but undisputed objective of which was
to enter into a near-catatonic stupor, with the prospect
of nursing a hangover the following morning an incon-
venient but indispensable part of the proceedings.

In fact, in terms of personality, Mark had much
more in common with his father than his contemporaries. For like Nicholas Newall he was a deep and
complex individual, and he chose to reveal his true
feelings to no one. An unusual blend of toughness
and tenderness, he was never really at ease rubbing
shoulders with the macho characters of the world of
beer and rugby. He had thus mastered the art of
concealing what might otherwise have been taken for
vulnerability or weakness. For underneath he was a
sensitive soul. As soon as his friend Nicholas's
mother had gone into hospital, for example, shortly
after the beginning of 1987, to continue her brave
battle against cancer, Mark's bouquet of flowers had

been among the first to arrive. Nicholas's mother, Corinne Symonds, remembers:

> That moved me a great deal. Because how many other nineteen-year-olds would have thought of such a kind and considerate gesture? It was a most beautiful and generous bouquet too. Although I could see that he was something of a loner, he was a most gentle and caring young man.

And yet at the same time Mark was drawn to the world of martial arts and all things eastern. He would occasionally hire the odd kung fu video and owned a martial arts device himself. He also derived great pleasure from reading true crime magazines, absorbing the detailed facts of strange and gruesome murders where the victims often met with an unusual, enigmatic or horribly violent death.

'Mark has a machiavellian mind,' is the view of Nan Clark. 'He works it all out. He weighs every word carefully. Just the opposite of Roderick. Mark is a thinker, whereas Roderick is much more likely to just open up his mouth and blurt something out.'

There was one occasion, though, when it was Mark who would have been better off keeping his lips sealed. With his parents spending most of their time at their villa in Spain, Mark alone was dealing with the negotiations for the sale of their house in Jersey, the spectacularly situated Crow's Nest at Grève de Lecq. For the most part he conducted himself well, emerging as a skilled negotiator with a fine grasp of detail. At one point during the transaction, however, there was a minor dispute about a piece of land that was supposed to be sold with the house. When it emerged that there might be a question mark over its ownership, Maureen Ellam, the prospective purchaser, immediately threatened to withdraw.

'If that land doesn't come with the house,' she informed the vendors' young representative, 'then I don't want it. It's as simple as that.'

'Mrs Ellam,' Mark had replied, his tone as haughty and arrogant as ever his father could be, 'I know that that land does belong to Crow's Nest. All I can say is that it's a question of gross incompetence on the part of my parents.'

Most infuriating of all for Maureen Ellam was the fact that Mark's assessment of his parents was entirely accurate. They had indeed been incompetent about staking their claim to the plot. But once he had seen to it that the appropriate remedial measures were taken, the conveyance had proceeded without further problems. Mark was pleased with the sale and proud to have been in the driver's seat throughout the transaction, which tends to be an extraordinarily complicated process in Jersey.

Shortly after the Ellams had moved into Crow's Nest, Mark dropped in to the Prince of Wales public house, situated just a few hundred yards away, to bid farewell to the publican there. Familiar both with the history and geography of the properties in the surrounding area, he was aware that some years earlier the publican had himself harboured various ambitious plans, including building a golf course and a large car park. It was all part of the aim of providing improved facilities for the growing number of people attracted to Grève de Lecq. At least that was the publican's argument to the planning committee. Together with every other local resident in the area, the Newalls had vociferously opposed the prospect of a major new development on their doorstep. But now that the Newalls' interest in the area had lapsed, Mark Newall felt at liberty to speak his mind.

'Right, you can do what you want to your field now,' he had announced to the publican. 'Keep pigs in it or whatever. Because we have just sold Crow's Nest for twice what it's worth.'

Even though the publican had been on the losing side of the battle with the island's powerful Development Committee, he did not appreciate Mark's remarks in the slightest, considering them precocious and offensive. Nor, when she heard of them, did Maureen Ellam. The next time the relevant parties were assembled together, she took advantage of the occasion to exact her revenge.

'Good,' she said, 'I'm glad I have got you all together. Because I would just like to ask you something, Mark. If your parents are such incompetent and grossly negligent people, then how come they have just managed to sell their house for twice what it is worth?'

Mark decided that the most effective response to this rather taxing question would be to absent himself, and promptly walked out of the room, which Maureen's husband David was already redesigning with dazzling results. But Nicholas was not prepared to let the matter of his son's indiscretion pass so easily.

'Maureen,' he fumed. 'Is that really true? Did Mark really say that?'

The new owner of Crow's Nest nodded, and cited her source in order to give her story further authority.

For a few seconds it appeared that Nicholas Newall was lost for words, a fate which did not often befall him. Then, quietly, he muttered: 'I really hate that boy.'

Nor was David Ellam Mark's most ardent admirer. 'He is just such an uppity little snot,' he would later explain, 'very much like his father in a way. But with Nick you knew that it was all just a front. That underneath he is a really nice person. The awful thing with Mark is that it's not a front at all. Because what you see is what you get.'

Mark Stephen Nelson Newall was born on 22 June 1966 at St Andrews, Scotland. But he was to be given precious little opportunity to develop truly Scottish roots, being whisked off on a boat *en route* to the West Indies before he had reached the age of two. It was largely because of his illness on board that his parents had decided to abandon their adventure, eventually settling in Jersey instead. Irene Stevenson, Mark's first teacher at the pre-prep school of St Michael's remembers his earliest days on the island:

I don't think there were any real problems outwardly, although I did notice that Mark was considerably more withdrawn than Roderick. I also remember making a note on his very first report that there had been quite a few signs of aggressive behaviour by him while at school, certainly sufficiently so for me to want to draw this to the attention of his parents.

'He was the most adorable, outgoing little boy,' his aunt, Nan Clark, is quick to counter:

Just look at the photographs. You could almost eat him up. He was cheeky, outgoing, handsome and delightful in every way. He was irrepressible, very bouncy and very smiley too. It was always a pleasure to have him in the house.

Mark soon found himself following in the footsteps of Roderick: Lockers Park, then Radley College, where he stepped into the new and at first rather bemused world of F Social. As he gradually settled into the school's routines, he began to particularly enjoy the Michaelmas term, when rugby is played and up to twenty teams might be fielded on any one day. Until he damaged his knee in a match, that is. It was such a severe injury that it marked the end of Mark's playing days, a disappointment which he took rather badly, and has obliged him ever since to wear a knee support while exercising. Indeed the accident was sufficiently serious for him to require brief in-patient treatment at Oxford's Radcliffe Infirmary.

Alerted to Mark's accident by the school, Elizabeth

Newall thought that his morale might receive a timely boost if he could be transferred to a private wing; that a little pampering might cheer him up considerably. But Nicholas Newall, still to visit his son, refused point blank. It was unthinkable that he should undertake expenditure of that kind. And when, a few days later, he heard that the injury was unlikely to cause any permanent damage or disability, he decided that he and Elizabeth could more usefully spend their time relaxing in Spain rather than visiting their son in Oxfordshire, and that is precisely what they did.

Like Roderick, Mark did not receive much love from his parents. Not that there was any discrimination against either boy in this respect. It was simply that the entire notion of paternal love was alien to Nicholas Newall. Having experienced a severely limited ration of it as a child, he had always concerned himself with a far more pragmatic aim: that his sons should grow up to be responsible adults, even if he sometimes shirked the odd responsibility himself.

'Mark just had no love from his parents,' Maureen Ellam insists.

> They really didn't like him. And you couldn't really like him either. Mark is pretty awful stuff. Whereas Elizabeth was quite fond of Roderick, she really didn't like Mark at all. Whenever he came up with something of which she disapproved she would throw her hands up in the air, feigning

despair, and exclaim: 'Oh, please, someone, take that awful boy away.'

An intelligent child, Mark had nevertheless managed to find love where it was not in such short supply. The youngest of her four grandsons, Mark was without doubt Elizabeth's mother's favourite. 'Granny Nelson' showered love and affection on Mark, and they became very close as a result. Nor did his feelings for her fade with the onset of adolescence. For not only would he dutifully remember all important occasions, he would regularly send to her in Scotland a bunch of flowers just to reaffirm his love.

Corinne Symonds recalls that:

He spoke about his mum and dad as and when they were coming and going, but without any real warmth. Because he hadn't received the love in order to be able to give it. That was my mother's instinct. I felt I needed to make up for the mothering he hadn't had in a way. Occasionally I would pat him on the arm and he would respond to that. But you were not allowed to get too close. Because suddenly he would withdraw again and decide that he was better off back in his shell. I actually felt very sorry for him. Eventually he was given a rather important job in Paris and as he prepared to leave we all started to fuss around him. Because as usual there was no back-up, no help, no support, nothing whatsoever, even though it was quite a big break in his career. As he was about to set off for the airport he was asked the predictable question: 'Have you got your passport?' Of course he hadn't. So really we all used to mother him all the time.

It was not that Mark's parents were incapable of demonstrating care and affection. Far from it. In fact they seemed to be able to come up with an ample supply when it came to nurturing their friendship with the Ellams. There would be birthday cards for Maureen and David, Christmas cards dispatched without fail, biscuits brought back for them from Scotland, and other small considerations besides.

To Angela Barnes, who had known the Newalls from their very first days on the island, the intensity of this new friendship was baffling. 'I just couldn't figure out this sudden enthusiasm for the Ellams,' she admits. 'Whatever the reasons for it, I couldn't help thinking that they showed far more consideration for them than they ever did towards their own children.'

Roderick and Mark might well have been competitive with each other as young boys and teenagers, but when it came to the wooing of women there was simply no match. For whereas Roderick's ebullient personality and striking good looks made him extremely attractive to very many women, Mark's more introverted nature brought him considerably less success. Not that it appeared to distress him unduly, and indeed to many it seemed as if sexual relationships hardly figured among his priorities. Mark spent very many evenings in the company of Nicholas Symonds's younger sister, Philippa. But there was never the slightest whiff of sexual chemistry in the air – only the pungent aroma of the Chinese take-away Mark would bring with him and tuck into before settling down for an uninterrupted evening of television at the Symonds's house.

Philippa Symonds explains:

> He wasn't one of the boys like the rest of my brother's friends. He was much more reserved altogether, not very fanciable at all really. I certainly never knew of any girlfriends as such, although there were platonic relationships with girls. I must say that it did cross my mind if he might not have been a little on the gay side. Not that he was effeminate in any way. Whatever the case, I don't think that he saw a lot of sexual activity of any kind.

Although the two brothers appeared to be establishing a much healthier relationship with one another, especially during the early summer of 1987, there remained a permanent undercurrent of tension between them. Indeed it was not very long before that, when they had attended a barbeque in Jersey together, that they had had a fist-fight and their friends had been obliged to keep them apart. To Corinne Symonds, who had observed both her son's and her daughter's relationships with him, Mark seemed to be very much in awe of his older brother, the tough, sporty and seductive soldier stationed on the mainland: 'Mark would often

say, "Oh, Rodders is coming over," and I couldn't help
feeling that he was a little bit wary of big brother. That
what he said went, and that Mark would end up by
having to toe the line. Even if that might not have been
convenient for him at all.'

If Roderick, with his hot head and quick temper, had
been cast in the same mould as Elizabeth, his mother,
then his younger brother, arrogant and acquisitive, and
always displaying a faint air of distant superiority, soon
learned to play the same games as his father. He
emerged as a younger Nicholas, and not a particularly
pleasant version at that.

'Mark really was a very cold fish,' recalls Natty
Ferreira, who cleaned for all the Newalls and had been
briefed by Elizabeth to keep a watchful eye on her
younger son. 'I used to do a bit of ironing for him as
well. But he never said a thank you. In fact he would
never say anything at all. He would just leave the
money out for me. I found him to be rather like Mr
Newall, very offish indeed.'

There was further common ground between father
and son, for both often struggled to conceal their
contempt for other people. But unlike his father, who
doted on Elizabeth, Mark felt only scorn for his
mother. It used to infuriate him when she would insist
on making contact by telephone during his working day
at Sheppards, suggesting that he might consider invest-
ing in this asset or that. He would be extremely curt
with her, insisting that she should not disturb him
again. Nor did the fact that his mother was simply
trying to discuss the deployment of her own funds

soften his attitude in any way. And when Nicholas would hear of his son addressing his mother so abruptly, at work or elsewhere, he did not like it at all. 'Don't treat your mother like that,' he would admonish him. 'You must have respect for her.'

'But Mark did not have an ounce of respect for his mother,' Angela Barnes confirms.

> He actually despised her. You could feel it in the air. There was always an atmosphere between them. He just used to treat her with utter contempt. Elizabeth used to think of herself as something of an academic. But Mark's view was that she was a blithering idiot. He thought that their lifestyle was frivolous. I remember the day when they heard that uncle Kenneth in Sark was going to bequeath a large amount of money to them before he died. Mark said: 'Huh, I can see what you two will do with it. You'll spend it and there won't be a penny left for Roderick and I.'

Perhaps it was because he sensed that there was an element of truth in his son's assertion, but even Nicholas appeared to be taken aback by the ferocity of Mark's onslaught.

'It's up to us what we do with our money,' he barked back.

It soon became clear that Nicholas's constant protestations that Mark ought to respect his mother had fallen on deaf ears. During the summer of 1986 an argument erupted over lunch at Angela Barnes's house. The row was sparked off by an issue of no great importance. Elizabeth had read a book and as she offered her interpretation of it, Mark made it quite clear that in his opinion his mother had entirely missed the point of the narrative. Tempers began to flare, Mark accusing his mother of being stupid and shallow. Never shy about speaking up for herself, Elizabeth fought back. The culmination of this bad-tempered exchange, each attack becoming more vicious by the minute, was that Mark threatened his mother. After a while Elizabeth could take no more. She got up from the table, went into the spare bedroom, and burst into tears. It was not the first time that Mark had spoken to her in such terms, and as she lay down and wept a string of equally acrimonious arguments from the past echoed in her mind.

'I don't know why you don't just leave them alone,' Maureen Ellam would later protest. 'They are lovely kids. Don't worry so much. They'll grow up soon enough. You should be pleased for Mark – that he is doing so well. Get off their backs.'

'Maureen,' Elizabeth had replied rather forlornly to her new-found friend. 'You don't know the half of it.'

5

'The Chances of Them Being Found Alive Are Very Slim'

She could scarcely conceal her enthusiasm. The whole world had to hear of Elizabeth's good news. The Newall family, more dispersed than ever now that Roderick and Mark had embarked on their respective careers in the military and high finance, was to be reunited after some time apart. It was to be a festive occasion too, with Elizabeth's forty-eighth birthday only a matter of a few days away; a time for celebration and champagne.

'Well, what *do* you think,' Elizabeth exclaimed to Maureen Ellam, her tone as bubbly and effusive as ever, 'those boys have come over to give me a special birthday surprise.'

It was true. Both sons had flown in from England on the evening of Friday 9 October 1987, six days before their mother's birthday. But with Roderick and Mark able to spend only the weekend on the island, the dinner was pencilled in for the Saturday night. No expense was to be spared. A table at one of Jersey's most stylish restaurants, that of the Sea Crest Hotel, was reserved. Situated on the secluded and picturesque bay of Petit Port, the restaurant rightfully enjoyed a reputation for its excellent food and was the perfect choice for an evening to remember.

But before the family party could get under way, there were several more mundane matters to attend to. Mark was anxious to hire a vehicle in which to transport some mattresses to his new home, La Falaise, at Noirmont. So he had set off shortly before lunch with his father to Falles Hire Cars, where they collected a red Renault van. It was typical of the sort of running about which Nicholas Newall had been doing ever since his return from Spain the previous August. He had been to the optician's the day before, he had recently undergone a series of tests in London about what he referred to as his ME, although it had never been diagnosed as such, and with Elizabeth he had spent the previous couple of months visiting relatives and friends in Scotland, Sark, London, Portsmouth and many places besides. A return to Javea, only ten days away, would undoubtedly be a return to tranquillity.

That Saturday also happened to be Maureen Ellam's birthday. The Newalls drove round to their former home at Grève de Lecq, intending to stay only a short while. But, as invariably happened when the two couples got together, the drinks began to flow and two hours slipped by almost unnoticed. Elizabeth and

Nicholas admired the Ellams for the major restructuring they were carrying out at Crow's Nest, transforming a rather dilapidated property into something quite spectacular. Here was a friendship which continued to flourish. For when the Newalls announced that they were likely to be spending an increasing amount of time on the island instead of Spain, Maureen Ellam's immediate reaction was to think of increasing the number of dinner dates together. 'Oh good,' the former publican enthused, 'that means that we'll be able to have two dinner parties a week instead of one.'

When, later that evening, Mark and Roderick returned to their parents' rather uninspiring bungalow, 9 Clos de L'Atlantique, they found a pre-dinner bottle of champagne cooled, ready and waiting. Since Mark had a habit of drinking little, and only vodka at that, it was agreed that his would be the safest pair of hands to drive the family to and from the restaurant. In the event, he reported that since his own car had refused to start that evening, he and Roderick had decided to travel from Noirmont to their parents' home in the red van he had hired earlier that day.

The restaurant did not disappoint the family. Having consumed a bottle of champagne in the hotel lounge, they were shown to table number seventeen by the restaurant manager, Paolo Corolla. As Mark went to take his seat the spring in his chair broke, causing a strange sensation in his backside. Quick-witted like his father, Mark took advantage of the situation to make a light-hearted joke about his sexuality – 'Ooh, I'm not that way inclined, you know' – and the offending chair was duly replaced. It was a particularly busy Saturday evening at the Sea Crest Hotel and Paolo went off to attend to other duties, leaving the Newalls in the very capable hands of Sergio Parmesan, an Italian waiter who has lived and worked in Jersey for over two decades. He recalls that evening clearly:

It was a lovely atmosphere that night at the restaurant. Mr and Mrs Newall sat with their backs to the window, with their sons sitting opposite them. The lady insisted that I knew her, from many years ago when I used to work at The Lobster Pot at L'Etacq in St Ouen. But I didn't. They had been in the previous August too. Then Mrs Newall had had *gambas* – big prawns – and she said that two of them were not right. I told her not to worry; that they would be all right on that Saturday night. But she actually chose lobster. Once her dish had arrived she complained about the colour of the lobster's claws. She said that they were rather too pink. I knew that the lobster had been cooked when she ordered it, so it was actually really fresh. A little later she then said that while it was very good, she had never seen a lobster with pink claws before. I replied that I had been serving fish for twenty years and I had seen plenty of lobsters with pink claws. I was beginning to get a bit fed up with all this because we were very busy. Then a couple from a neighbouring table stepped in to say that the lobster had pink claws because it had been fished in deep waters. That seemed to settle the matter, thank goodness, and Mrs Newall appeared to be happy about it.

Throughout the evening Mark stuck to his teetotal guns, alternating between Coke and mineral water while his parents and brother consumed still more champagne and three bottles of wine. After dessert had been served and with the time fast approaching midnight the Newalls returned to the hotel lounge. There was time for one last drink, and Roderick and Nicholas ordered whiskies from the bar. The bill came to a little over £130, which Mark paid for with his Access card. The evening seemed to have gone smoothly enough, although the restaurant manager noticed that Roderick seemed to have a very tense air about him. He was certainly not as relaxed-looking as his brother, who was also much smarter in appearance.

Just as Elizabeth was emerging from the ladies room, she bumped into Sergio Parmesan again. It was another opportunity for her to comment on one of the evening's dishes, although this time not her own. 'Oh, by the way,' she said, 'two of the *gambas* were not right again.' Then Mark approached. As her son came within earshot, Elizabeth hurriedly instructed the waiter not to say anything to him, for the meal had been a birthday treat and the last thing she would wish to do was to offend either of her sons in any way. What nobody appeared to notice, however, was that the lobster, the colour of whose claws had been debated at some length, had been omitted from the bill.

With Mark at the wheel of his father's new silver-grey Citroën, the Newalls set off on the short journey back home. Their arrival was the cue for a nightcap of Macallan, an eighteen-year-old malt whisky. All in all it had been a thoroughly enjoyable evening out.

Shortly before nine o'clock the following morning Maureen Ellam left Crow's Nest in her VW estate car for Jersey's airport, situated in the parish of St Peter. Her brother was flying in from the mainland, as the islanders refer to it, and was due to land within the hour. Even so, she felt confident that if she moved at a spritely pace she would have just enough time to pop into the Newalls on the way. She had received a number of bouquets for her own birthday and thought that it would be a nice gesture to give one to Elizabeth. Besides, she had a couple of other items which she wanted to return to the Newalls before their scheduled departure for Spain on 20 October.

Placing the bouquet on the doorstep, Maureen rang the bell and without waiting for a response, began to make her way back to her car. 'As I did so the door opened and it was Roderick. I said, "Oh, what's this, then, the young up before the old?" '

Roderick replied that his parents were still asleep.

Maureen recalls:

'Really?' I said. By then I had walked over and was close to him. 'Christ,' I said, 'that was some night, wasn't it?' I meant drinking, of course, because he really looked dissipated. There was a bit of chit-chat as I handed him the flowers. Then I

Murder victim Nicholas Newall living the good life in Spain

Elizabeth Newall at 9 Clos de L'Atlantique, the bungalow in which she and her husband were subsequently killed

Aunt Nan Clark with her nephews Roderick and Mark (front) at Martello Cottage in 1969

Roderick and Mark were engaging little boys

Handsome, healthy and mischievous, the Newall boys had more than their fair share of scraps together

Roderick after his passing-out parade at Sandhurst, pictured with his parents

Roderick in military attire with his mother

Mark with Nan Clark at a family wedding in Scotland in 1990

Roderick loved sailing and took every opportunity to use the family yacht when visiting their holiday home in Spain

Roderick during his army career, a dashing soldier who charmed the girls

Searching for clues in the garden of 9 Clos de L'Atlantique during the five long and frustrating years when precious little progress was made on the Newall case (*Jersey Evening Post*)

The Sea Crest Hotel where the family celebrated Elizabeth's forty-eighth birthday on Saturday 10 October 1987. A few hours after their lobster and champagne dinner both Elizabeth and Nicholas were murdered in their home

said: 'Still asleep, go on, put them on her bed. When she opens her eyes she will think that she has died.' It wasn't a bit funny to Roderick. As I left the house I thought that that boy should never wear red. I thought, asleep? They wouldn't be asleep. Why did he say that? That all flashed through my mind. But then I thought, I know, he has said that they are asleep because I am a noisy and pushing little female at nine o'clock on a Sunday morning. Maybe he thought that I wanted to get in to see his parents, which wasn't the case at all. So everything seemed perfectly acceptable to me. I then said to Roderick: 'Right, now watch me get lost between here and the airport.' And off I went.

When Maureen returned to Crow's Nest, she immediately asked her husband if Elizabeth had phoned. She knew that the chances were that her friend would already have been in touch, because Elizabeth always found it difficult to resist picking up the phone at the best of times. To her, whether or not there was a precise reason for ringing someone was rather a secondary issue. It was only a matter of time, therefore, before she would call, full of warmth and enthusiasm as always, and in this particular instance thanking her friend for the flowers. Yet as the day wore on that telephone call appeared to be quite some time in coming. Eventually Maureen dialled Elizabeth's number herself: three times on the Monday, four times on the Tuesday. But each time the phone just rang and rang. She struggled hard to come up with a compelling reason why there was no reply.

It was easy enough to account for the boys. Mark and Roderick had both left the island for the mainland late that Sunday afternoon, having taken separate flights within half an hour of each other. In fact Mark had tried and failed to get his car on to the ferry, so he had left his sporty Toyota, which he had evidently managed to get started, at the airport car park instead, intending to return for it a couple of days later. Whatever the case, it was clear that neither son had been in the house to pick up the phone.

As the early part of the following week went by the Newalls began to miss a number of appointments. It was all very mysterious. Elizabeth had been due to meet David Ellam on the Monday; he was going to help her select some coving for her sitting room. The Newalls knew that even a fraction of the Ellams' flair would do wonders for their new and more modest property situated within the parish of St Brelade, and which they referred to as their *pied-à-terre*. The following day a lunch appointment was missed. Still there had been no phone call. And still there was no reply. The Newalls had been due to visit Uncle Kenneth on Sark on the Wednesday, the last opportunity to see him before their departure for Spain. But they did not turn up there either. Apart from anything else Maureen was wondering when she would be able to personally deliver her birthday card to her dear friend Elizabeth, whose forty-eighth birthday was the following day.

'I was beginning to get anxious,' Maureen admits. 'I had bought one of those cards that plays *Happy Birthday* as it opens. By now I had become rather worried. Alarm bells were beginning to ring. I kept saying the same thing to David: "Where the bloody hell are they?" '

During the night of Thursday 15 October Jersey took a battering the likes of which it had not experienced since the hurricane of 1964. Winds of up to a hundred miles per hour lashed the island in the early hours, leaving a trail of damage and chaos in their wake. Whole roofs were ripped off buildings, granite walls crumbled like sandcastles, dozens of cars were crushed by trees brought tumbling to the ground by storm-force winds which had apparently taken the weather forecasters entirely by surprise. It was a wild and chaotic night, bringing down overhead cables and telegraph poles, and tossing boats around at St Helier, St Aubin and Gorey as if they were toys. A fireman was rushed to Jersey's General Hospital at St Helier with injuries to his skull after being struck by a falling tree at Clos des Sables. And in a separate incident two children, Tatania and Adam Wavell, narrowly escaped injury when a chimney stack crashed through the roof of their bedroom. It was a night which most of Jersey's inhabitants are unlikely to forget.

As calls to the emergency services reached a peak and the extent of the great storm became clear, the police braced themselves for daybreak, when they expected to find not just devastation and serious injuries, but perhaps a substantial number of fatalities too.

'It was a miracle that no one was killed,' Chief Officer Bob Le Breton recalls.

The following day there was a frenetic attempt to restore some semblance of order and normality to the island. As this was taking place, Maureen Ellam was still wondering what on earth could have happened to her friends. The storm might well have wreaked havoc in Jersey, but it at least suggested a possible explanation. Perhaps Elizabeth and Nicholas had succeeded in making their way to Sark after all, but had now found themselves stranded there, incommunicado, because of the devastating impact of the storm.

This theory, however, could not be sustained for very long. For Elizabeth and Nicholas Newall had been due to dine with the Ellams that Friday night, by which time Sark's telephone system was fully operational again. Besides, almost an entire week had now elapsed since the family gathering at the Sea Crest Hotel. Maureen knew that the time had come to act. She phoned Paul Shearer, next-door neighbour to the Newalls. He reported that the storm had ripped a few tiles from the roof of their house, but there had been no activity there for the best part of a week. Certainly their Citroën had not budged an inch. When Maureen asked the young man if he would mind knocking on their door, he was happy to oblige. He knew very well that there was unlikely to be any reply and there was not. Then, curious himself, he jumped over an adjoining wall and approached the back of the 9 Clos de L'Atlantique with its rather neglected drab brown paintwork. Before attempting to enter the bungalow, however, he thought that it might be wise to ask his friend, Chris Poirrier, who happened to be visiting him, to accompany him. Paul certainly felt more confident about investigating together, but both men were now beginning to wonder exactly what they might find.

They soon realized that no training in the more sophisticated techniques of housebreaking was called for, since the verandah's sliding doors were open. As they stepped inside cautiously, the first thing both young men noticed, apart from the fact that nobody else appeared to be at home, was that the bungalow seemed to be exceedingly hot. That apart, there was apparently nothing remarkable to report. Unopened mail lay on the floor; the ironing board was set up and ready for use; in the kitchen there was a jar of marmalade, oatcakes and sugar on the table, and milk, eggs and bacon in the fridge; the master bedroom was not particularly tidy; Nicholas's shaving gear was in the house, as were the couple's tooth-brushes. There was washing on the line – surely another indication that the Newalls had not expected to be away for very long. Certainly Paul did not know what to make of it. Not that he had ever had much to do with the Newall family, for they were relative newcomers to the estate who lived abroad for most of the year and who in any event always kept themselves to themselves.

By this time David Ellam wanted to see for himself what was going on. Unlike Paul Shearer, he had no need even to contemplate a possible break-in, for he had a front-door key. He too was struck by the stifling heat in the bungalow, and soon saw that the thermo-static control had been overridden so as to leave the heating permanently on high. He turned it off immediately. There had been a bout of bad weather, true enough, David thought, but overall it had been a fairly mild autumn and had certainly not warranted such a searing heat. He also knew that his wife was anxious to phone Mark, but had been unable to do so, having been told his Noirmont number was ex-directory. However, it was soon found at the bungalow.

Maureen dialled the five-digit Jersey number, hoping that Mark might be able to unravel the mystery. Having had many dealings with him in the past, most notably during the Ellams' purchase of his parents' former home at Grève de Lecq, she knew that he was a capable young man, despite the tension that followed the sale. After a couple of rings the Euro-bond dealer picked up the telephone not in Jersey but London. This unremarkable example of modern technology threw Maureen off her track. Instead of immediately asking about Mark's parents she became more interested in how he had been able to arrange to receive his calls in London, before returning to the matter in hand.

'Love, it's rather out of character,' she said, 'but something has happened to your parents. Your mother has never gone for more than twenty-four hours without phoning me – and they were due to dine with us at Victoria's last night. Got any clues?'

'Well no, Mrs Ellam,' Mark replied, courteous and respectful as always.

'I know that you were here last weekend. Do you

know what their plans were for the week?'

Together they ran through the appointments they knew of. Everything appeared to tally. It was clear that a number of other engagements had also been missed.

'He was super-helpful,' Maureen recalls.

> He told me that the four of them had lunched together at home on the Sunday after their meal at the Sea Crest Hotel, and that both he and Roderick had left the island later that afternoon. But it was clear to me that since he had no idea at all as to their likely whereabouts the time had come to call the police.

In fact both sons were themselves now expressing the greatest concern. Ever since Maureen's call Mark had been frantically telephoning relatives and friends in England, Spain and Scotland – anyone, in fact, with whom he thought his parents might have made contact. Always able to control his emotions, he was brief and to the point. Seldom did his question vary. Had his parents been in touch? But the answer did not vary either. No, they had not.

On Sunday 18 October, eight days after the Newalls' family gathering at the Sea Crest Hotel, Roderick returned to Jersey, the first son to return. Mark had already altered his arrangements so as to be able to go back to the island too. The Ellams picked Roderick up at the airport and together they made their way to the States of Jersey police headquarters at Rouge Bouillon, having first called in at the bungalow at Clos de

L'Atlantique. A grim task now awaited them: to officially report Elizabeth and Nicholas Newall as missing. The three of them still had no idea why the couple should have suddenly vanished from the face of the earth. No message had been left. The house had been left open, with the heating on full blast. It was all very unsettling. Perhaps the police would be able to come up with a few answers.

The approach of the police could hardly have been more clear-cut. Since there appeared to be no evidence at all that a crime had been committed, it was simply a case of missing persons. Graham Nimmo explains:

> I happened to be the only operational Detective Inspector in Jersey at that time, and therefore this case rather fell into my lap. And into Jimmy Adamson's too, since he was my sergeant at the time. I sat in that lounge at Clos de L'Atlantique for many an hour. The scene-of-crime people were also there for a long time. As far as we were concerned it was an extremely good scene. You have to remember that there had been the storm. Life on the island had been completely disrupted. Two people had gone missing. So why should we, in the first week, suspect any foul play? That would have been an unfair assumption to make. And yet at the same time I felt deeply uneasy; I sensed that something was wrong.

So did Maureen Ellam. Within a few days of the disappearance of her friends, she had begun to feel that there were sufficient suspicious circumstances to justify calling in a team of forensic experts. Where was the black hearth rug which was normally in front of the fire? What had happened to the stain on the carpet in Elizabeth and Nicholas's bedroom, a mark which she had earlier pointed out to Roderick, assuming it to be tea or coffee, but which appeared to have been speedily washed away? And what was the atmosphere that had prompted her to say to Roderick while standing in the lounge of the bungalow: 'This house feels wrong'? Habitually frank and forthright, she complained loudly about the length of time the police were taking before bringing in specialist officers.

'Mrs Ellam,' came the reply, 'we are dealing with two missing persons and nothing more. There has been no crime for us to investigate.'

Not that the police had been inactive. On the contrary, within forty-eight hours of Roderick reporting his parents as missing Superintendent Bob Le Breton had ordered that a major incident room be set up – hardly standard procedure in a missing persons inquiry. And while the attitude of the Royal Green Jackets officer appeared to be one of genuine bewilderment and concern, he certainly failed to come across as eager to cooperate with police personnel, even on his first visit to Rouge Bouillon.

'And how would you describe your mother, Mr Newall,' Roderick was asked by a young PC whose job it was to take down as many details as possible.

'Jolly hockey-sticks,' came the reply, without a moment's hesitation.

'And your mother's voice?'

'Could you possibly give me a few adjectives from which to choose?'

Aware that Roderick was out to intimidate the woman police constable with a rather condescending, if polished, display of irony, Maureen Ellam rebuked him and promptly provided a suitable epithet herself. 'Excitable,' she suggested.

Mark's approach appeared to be a little out of the ordinary too. That at least was the view of his Aunt Nan, who had by now made her way back to Jersey from Spain with her husband Alister. She had reason to feel uneasy about her sister's disappearance. For barely a week had elapsed since her appalling nightmare in which Elizabeth and Nicholas had met a gruesome fate. As Nan Clark began to carefully retrace her own and her sister's steps, she realized that her horrific dream of Elizabeth had occurred an hour or so after the family meal at the Sea Crest Hotel.

Alister and I went straight to the police station. We waited a short time and then on leaving the reception office to go over to the other side of the building across a quadrangle we encountered Mark. He seemed very tense and withdrawn. I didn't throw my arms around him or hug him because I thought he would break down. In fact I thought we both would. As we were going up the stairs Mark said to me: 'Stephen [Newall] says don't tell the police about the two sets of passports.' I didn't know that they had two sets of passports, but this remark struck me as rather odd as the very first thing to say to your aunt in the circumstances. But then again shock can make you act very strangely.

Roderick had also said something which had given his aunt cause for concern even before her return to Jersey. It had preyed on her mind ever since. 'I don't think there is any hope,' he had announced rather grimly in the first of a series of telephone conversations between them. In fact it was this comment that had prompted the Clarks to pack their bags and set off on the long haul from Spain to Jersey.

Nan Clark explains:

From what I had heard I couldn't understand why he should have said this. After all, they had only gone missing. And as if all of this was not enough to contend with, I then also had my own mother on the line complaining that Roderick was in Jersey all alone in the house at Clos de L'Atlantique with no one there to look after him. Was he eating enough, she wanted to know. Yes, I assured her, he had had baked beans on toast.

Detective Inspector Graham Nimmo knew that it was imperative to organize a search, to comb the island as thoroughly as possible. The coastline and sand dunes of La Moye were singled out as areas worthy of close inspection, and the French coastal rescue service Crossma was contacted to see if their help might be available. Yet as these arrangements were being finalized, Graham Nimmo had something else on his mind:

Within five minutes of meeting these boys, and I mean five minutes, I knew that there was something wrong. I spoke to them both on the first day that they were back on the island. I spoke to them in that same lounge, and I wanted to speak to them separately. Roderick was in the kitchen, but he couldn't keep himself out of the room – he kept wanting to come back in to find out what his brother was saying. He just kept interrupting, he couldn't keep away. So eventually I insisted that he did. Their stories were consistent enough, but then again they had had a lot of time to get it right, over a week in fact. I saw guilt in their eyes as soon as I met them. Jimmy Adamson agreed with me totally. Roderick was extremely nervous. His tummy muscles were contracting so much that it affected his neck. Plus he had been drinking as well. I didn't trust a single word either of them said. Of course you couldn't say so directly though. In fact we were very sympathetic towards them at first. After all it was they who had reported to us that their parents were missing. So it was a kind of chess game which we were obliged to pursue. Call it intuition if you like, but my copper's nose told me that there was something very wrong with these two boys.

Acting Chief Inspector Paul Marks was standing in the

lounge of the Newalls' home, the detectives having asked him to carry out a detailed search of the bungalow, when suddenly he breathed a sigh of relief. 'Oh, you're back then,' he said, embarrassed to be surprised in the house but now confident that the case was about to be closed. Having studied the photographs and particulars of the Newalls closely, he knew right away that the man who had just walked through the front door fitted the description of Nicholas Newall. 'No, I'm Nicholas's twin brother, Stephen,' the man replied. 'We do look alike though.'

Stephen Newall had travelled down from Scotland to see if he might not be able to assist in some way. He had checked into the four-star Atlantic Hotel at La Moye, just a few hundred yards from the Newalls' bungalow. In fact both Roderick and Mark eventually reserved rooms for themselves there too, as did Nan and Alister. Then Granny Nelson flew in from Scotland in a distressed state yet anxious to be on the spot and with other members of the family. Only Stephen Newall seemed to be relatively relaxed about the whole affair. He was in quite high spirits, joking and chatting happily enough with his two nephews, with whom he had always got on well. He felt confident that the matter would be resolved within a matter of days, and indicated that he would not be able to remain on the island for long.

Nan Clark remembers the arrival of another visitor:

A girlfriend from Paris, Elena, a very tall and most striking girl then joined our party at the Atlantic

Hotel. She was working in the same office as Mark. I was never quite sure whose girlfriend she was. All the time the police were coming in and out of the hotel taking statements. And there we all were: two presentable young men, a pretty young lady, granny, aunt and uncle. Then a television crew came into the hotel to film the latest episode of *Bergerac* at the bar while we were sitting there. There was also an art exhibition being held at the hotel at that time, so Elizabeth's friends were coming and going all the time. This is the only time in my life that I have ever felt like something out of an Agatha Christie novel, sitting in the palm court of an expensive hotel. It was almost unreal.

Angela Barnes was one of those friends who popped into the Atlantic Hotel. Like Graham Nimmo and Maureen Ellam, she was deeply suspicious of the boys. After all, she had heard of dire threats and fighting within the Newall family for more years than she cared to remember. More than any other person on the island, she had seen the writing on the wall:

I had a pretty good idea of what might have happened. In fact I sat and talked with Mark at the Atlantic Hotel after dinner one evening during the week after the disappearance. Everything seemed to be very jolly and gay. Mark came in with an enormous bunch of flowers for Granny Nelson. He then said that his parents would be away for just a

few days. I asked him how he knew. He replied
that he knew what clothes were missing. So I said
to Mark: 'What about the dark suit which Nicholas
was wearing at the Sea Crest that night?' It had a
faint check and a dramatic bright-red silk lining. I
said: 'I wonder if he has got that with him.'
Whereupon Mark went white. But I didn't want to
be rude to either of the boys, so I just pretended
that everything was normal.

By now the search for Elizabeth and Nicholas Newall
was well under way. It had begun with both States of
Jersey and honorary police making their way through
the Five Mile Road area. Then searches of the coastal
walks in St Ouen, St Peter and St Brelade were carried
out with the help of the Fire Service inshore rescue
boat. The impact of the recent storm made these
attempts all the more difficult and hazardous. Meanwhile, as extensive house-to-house inquiries continued
apace, hundreds of posters were being printed for
distribution around the island. A detailed description
of the clothing thought to have been worn by the
Newalls was released in the hope that members of the
public might be able to help. Before long hundreds of
people had been interviewed, so that statements began
to pile up on top of one another in the incident room
and a manual reference-card system was likewise soon
packed with information. It was all very useful in
building up an overall picture of the Newalls.

But still there had been no positive sighting of the
couple. The only option was to press on with the

search. Ouaisné Bay, Sorrel Point and the Grève de Lecq area were inspected at close quarters. Even the refuse heap at La Saline was examined, albeit with the help of a mechanical digger. And then a number of septic tanks, cesspits and boreholes were earmarked as other sites worthy of close scrutiny. Despite their best efforts and the involvement of large numbers of police personnel, those responsible for bringing the case to a swift and successful conclusion emerged from these further investigations none the wiser.

'I have dug more holes in this island than I ever dug in my own back garden all my life,' Graham Nimmo confesses. And all to no avail. During the first few weeks after the disappearance of his parents, Mark Newall occasionally made himself available to reporters. Each time he was interviewed, his theme was one of bafflement, as when he said:

> If you look at the available facts in a logical way they do not fit any of the theories of an accident, kidnap, suicide or murder, and therefore the odds are that something illogical has happened to them. It's just totally out of character. It's never happened before. For my mother to be out of contact for more than five or six days would be considered extremely unusual. It just doesn't make any sense.

It was precisely because none of it did seem to make any sense that rumours began to sweep through the island concerning the fate of the Newalls. Every islander appeared to have his or her own theory. There was talk of the Mafia; of the hiring of professional hit men; of a left-hand-drive pink Mercedes saloon bearing foreign number plates and supposed to have been seen outside the bungalow at Clos de L'Atlantique but which could no longer be accounted for; of the Newalls having engineered their own disappearance *à la* Lord Lucan; of criminal connections in Spain and, inevitably perhaps, of illicit trafficking in drugs.

Those who took the view that the Newalls were unlikely to be found alive allowed their imaginations to work overtime. Numerous locations where their bodies were likely to be found were mentioned, each one more fanciful than the next. Some people were convinced that the couple had been buried at the golf course at La Moye, just a stone's throw from their bungalow. Others preferred to plump for Portelet Common as the most likely spot. Another faction pressed the case for their having been buried at sea, while a small but vociferous minority pointed ominously towards the Bellazone incinerator. People purporting to be experts on the Newall case appeared to pop up, as if from nowhere, almost every day. All this was taking place when the simple truth was that nobody knew anything at all.

It was in this atmosphere of frenzied speculation and confusion that the States of Jersey police invited Brian Terris, a Guernsey psychic, to have his say. Planning to use a technique known as radiesthesia, he headed off towards Portelet Common accompanied by two police officers and armed with maps, compasses, magnets and a pendulum. A member of the British Society of Dowsers, his techniques might well have been out of the ordinary, yet they had been instrumental in discovering the body of a Guernsey resident, Lorraine Vaudin, during the course of the previous summer. However, Terris's pendulum now began to swing in a cross pattern, indicating only a confused situation.

'A bloodhound picks up a scent but he gets confused. That's what happened to me. Maybe I've overworked on this case. I've been under a lot of pressure. I think I must have got tired and lost the thread. I do hope that this couple are still alive though.'

With those words the disappointed psychic returned to Guernsey, obliging the police to return to more conventional methods of detection.

Nan Clark's approach was much more down to earth. She too had spent some time walking around the island looking for clues. An experienced businesswoman with a keen eye for detail, she had been thinking about a cashmere sweater which Roderick had been wearing. Her sister had bought a number of these in Scotland with a view to taking them back to Spain, where they are much sought after by the sizeable British expatriate community. Nan Clark explains:

Elizabeth had shown these cashmere sweaters to me when we were in London together just a few weeks previously. She had bought them for friends in Spain. I was very surprised to see Roderick wearing one of them. I didn't think he would have dared to do this if he thought that Elizabeth was going to come back. So that made me feel a little uneasy. I thought that the boys knew more than they were letting on. But certainly nothing more ominous than that.

She began to feel considerably more uneasy, however, when she returned to the bungalow with Detective Inspector Nimmo and Sergeant Adamson. Standing with his back to the fireplace, the latter, himself a Scot, picked up the poker and immediately handed it to his boss. On its tip there was a dark-red stain which looked as if it might well be congealed blood. Immediately Graham Nimmo arranged to have the poker sent to the laboratory, where it would be subjected to rigorous scientific examination.

'I suspected the boys,' he says.

But we did not have much to go on. We did a lot of undercover stuff to try to find out more. Because none of us were satisfied with what they were saying. We soon found ourselves working with a huge police team, some thirty or forty people working full-time on the case. We went to Scotland. We went to Sark. We went to Spain. We did everything we could. But the fact of the matter was that we had not found any bodies. In my own mind I had come to the conclusion that we were dealing with a double murder inquiry. It's one thing to suspect murder though, and quite another to prove it. And we couldn't prove it. It was as simple as that.

A headline in the *Jersey Evening Post* appeared to sum up the position rather well: 'Police admit they are baffled.' It was true. If a double murder had been committed, as an increasing number of people were beginning to suspect, then there had not been much progress at all. No motive had been produced. No bodies had been found. No arrests had been made; nor were any envisaged in the immediate future. it was hardly a resounding success for Graham Nimmo and his team. Frustration was setting in, and at the time Maureen Ellam admitted:

I'm angry that the police can't find them if they have been murdered. It's such a little island. You can't bury fourteen and twelve stone easily and not leave a trace, can you? They had no real enemies. Elizabeth was a beautiful woman. To think of her rotting in some dirty corner – that is what angers me. They deserve more. This case should be solved.

And while the word 'murder' never passed their lips – at least in relation to their own involvement in the mysterious disappearance of their parents – as the weeks and months went by both Roderick and Mark seemed to accept the notion that they were unlikely ever to return. Mark, the spokesman for them both ever since they were small boys, appeared on television to state their position. Now he too seemed to hold out little hope: 'There is absolutely no reason whatsoever for my parents to go without leaving word. People just don't disappear and then walk through the door a few weeks later and say, "Hi, folks." So if we are to look at it realistically, then the chances of them being found alive are very slim.'

6

Parricide Perfected?

Mark Newall was right: the chances of his parents being
alive were slim indeed. For Dr David Northcott, a
Home Office scientist called in from the mainland to
assist in the inquiry, was able to find blood at the
bungalow whereas the local police had not. So much
blood, in fact, that he had no difficulty at all in
concluding that both Elizabeth and Nicholas Newall
had been murdered in their home some time between
10 and 17 October 1987. His discovery left him in not
the slightest doubt that an episode of sustained violence
had taken place at the bungalow. And, as a result, what
had begun initially as a missing persons inquiry turned
into the longest and most intense double-murder investigation in Jersey's history.

The cleaning of the family home had been so thorough that traces of the Newalls' blood were barely

visible to the naked eye. For the expert from the Forensic Laboratory at Aldermaston, however, there was no shortage of evidence of foul play. The clean-up had been good. But not good enough.

The stain which Maureen Ellam had noticed by the door of her friends' bedroom, and which she had assumed to be tea or coffee, might well have been removed. But there had been so much spillage that another stain, measuring four and a half by two and a half inches, lay beneath both the carpet and underlay on the parquet flooring. It was neither spilt tea or coffee, but blood belonging to the same group as that of Elizabeth Newall. There were also a number of tiny specks of blood around the door frame. The scene in the bedroom indicated that she had died there, having received multiple blows as she was attempting to make her way out of the room.

In the lounge there was evidence of further violence. For between the drinks cabinet and the television and to the right of the fireplace were found an ample supply of tiny pinpricks of blood belonging to the same group as Nicholas Newall.

'At some stage someone was lying on the carpet long enough to lose a large quantity of blood,' Dr Northcott explains, 'because it was sprayed quite widely on the walls, right up to the ceiling.'

Just as in the bedroom, it had seeped through to the parquet flooring below. Here, in front of the fireplace, was the spot where the retired fifty-six-year-old Scottish schoolteacher and Lloyds name had met his death. Fibres taken away for analysis revealed that a green scouring pad had been used to clean up. But despite the intense scrubbing which had taken place almost every black object in that room also had minute traces of blood on it. The poker by the fireplace had indeed revealed blood, as both Graham Nimmo and Jimmy Adamson had suspected at the outset. But since it was just a speck the poker was presumed not to have been the murder weapon.

In the bathroom there was further evidence of bloodshed: in the basin, shower and bath areas; on the scrubbing brush near where the cleaning utensils were kept; at the hand-towel area; on the shampoo bottles. Traces of blood were found in all of these places.

It was clear that several hours had been spent cleaning up. That in itself was rather baffling, for not many killers while away the hours with shine and polish after carrying out their crime. Even the duvet cover in the master bedroom had been laundered, albeit rather crudely since it appeared to have been put back on to the bed damp. There were also spots of blood on the wall under the kitchen table, which gave the impression that it had been shifted when the bodies were moved. And not only was the black hearth rug missing, as Maureen Ellam had noticed, but so were other items from the mantelpiece, including a number of books. Towels had likewise disappeared from the bathroom, evidently part of the meticulous cleaning-up operation which had taken place.

Here, then, was the reason why the heating had been left on so high and for so long: to help dry out the bungalow, which for a few hours at least, had been literally dripping with blood. Here at last was over-whelming evidence that Elizabeth and Nicholas Newall had been brutally murdered in their own home. Devoted to one another if not to their sons, they had met their deaths just a couple of months before their silver wedding anniversary.

Armed with this powerful new evidence, the police immediately renewed contact with Roderick, who by now had returned to his regiment in the Royal Green Jackets, although he remained eager to leave the Army. Not surprisingly, they were anxious to take a further statement from him. But initially he refused, on the grounds that the police had broken a promise that he would be allowed to have access to previous state-ments. His brother's approach was rather different: on learning from the police that a major murder inquiry had been launched, he immediately set about arranging a reward. Within a few weeks he revealed that he was in a position to be able to offer £40,000 for information leading to the arrest and conviction of those responsible for the savage slaughter of his parents.

Roderick Newall might well have been reluctant to co-operate with Detective Inspector Graham Nimmo. But other witnesses were coming forward, and slowly an increasing amount of circumstantial evidence began to accumulate, for the most part pointing the finger at the Newall sons themselves. Their version of events, however, remained entirely consistent: that after the family meal at the Sea Crest Hotel on 10 October they had left their parents' home in the early hours and travelled together to spend the night at Mark's new home near Noirmont, returning to the bungalow at Clos de L'Atlantique at approximately eight-thirty the next morning. They had said goodbye to their parents after enjoying a typical family Sunday lunch. It was an explanation which could hardly have been more innocent or straightforward-seeming.

Then cracks in the brothers' stories began to appear. Sheila Cruickshank, who lived next door to Mark's new home, reported that from her entrance-hall window she had seen both a red van and a white Toyota car. The boot and doors of both vehicles were open and she had been able to see two young men passing articles to each other, although she was unable to say from which vehicle to which. What she was quite sure about, however, was the time, having been woken up at six o'clock on that Sunday morning by the sound of slamming doors, an abrupt and early awakening which had not pleased her at all. And then a Mrs Maureen Bickerton revealed to police that two men had come to her front door at two o'clock that Sunday afternoon asking where they might be able to burn some rubbish. They too had a red van.

The brothers' claim to have been lunching with their parents was looking increasingly unlikely. More damning still was the fact that, although it took the police some time to track down and eventually repossess the red Falles hire van, when they did so they found further traces of blood. In addition, a similar Renault van was seen driving around the north of the island. It was hardly surprising that neither son was eager to face Graham Nimmo and his team.

Although Nan Clark had initially been protective towards her nephews, she now began a slow and painful process of realization that Roderick and Mark might well have been involved in some way. Part of her began to admit the unthinkable: that the two small boys whom she had watched grow up into fine young men, and whom she loved dearly, might indeed be sharing a guilty secret. At the same time another part of her mind quickly fought back, dismissing such a notion as preposterous and assuring her that they were not. Her diary records:

2.2.88 Nimmo showed photographs of house and showed us press statement. Boys still refused blood samples. Le Breton lost his temper with them. R + M still determined to niggle at police and accuse them of time wasting and inefficiency. M very edgy. R calm but argumentative. Crown Advocate is going through statements. Later M slightly improved but very quiet. Met Nimmo, Le Brocq and Adamson. Discussed possible suspects. We agreed to return to give blood in hope this would encourage boys. Le Breton says he might have to halt enquiry because of lack of funds if boys did not co-operate and give blood and access to accounts. The police still say evidence points to the boys.

Nor was Stephen Newall impressed with the behaviour of his nephews. He had not hesitated to assist the police in any way that he could. Indeed it had been his readiness to provide a blood sample that had enabled the forensic team at Aldermaston to be able to confirm that the blood found in the lounge was his brother Nicholas's. That had been one of the more straightforward forensic tests, since twins always share the same blood group. So why were Roderick and Mark not prepared to do likewise and assist the police in their inquiries? He knew that there could only be one reason: they had something to hide.

Aware of the importance of finding Elizabeth and Nicholas's bodies in order for there to be a satisfactory conclusion to the case, the police redoubled their efforts. Sewers were searched. So too was Jersey's vast network of underground German bunkers and military installations dating from the Occupation. Over twenty calls were received in response to a broadcast on BBC television's *Crimewatch UK*. But they were for the most part supposed sightings of the couple, and all came to nothing. Then the police turned their attention to the Newalls' garden. A scientist was flown over from the mainland to examine the forty by fifty-foot plot with sub-surface radar equipment. Before long the sophisticated technology had yielded a signal which was analysed, digitized and then processed by a computer which in turn produces a video image. However, despite the use of the most modern techniques, at a cost of several thousand pounds, no images at all were provided by the equipment. It was another disappointing day for the police, one of many which they were to experience in the weeks and months ahead.

Then, in March 1988, Roderick was suddenly arrested. It was hardly the breakthrough for which the police had been hoping. Having recently resigned his commission in the Royal Green Jackets, the handsome former lieutenant had been travelling on a flight from Southampton to Jersey. Once the plane had landed all passengers had been asked to wait in one of the holding lounges in the airport's passenger pier while two dogs trained in drug detection work examined hand baggage. It was the first time that such an operation had been launched. A small quantity of cannabis was found among Roderick's belongings. He was detained and taken to police headquarters at Rouge Bouillon.

A few weeks later the family's lawyer, David Le Quesne, submitted to the Police Court the information that his client had used the substance merely as a form of relaxation, and embarked on a powerful plea of mitigation. It was a way of coping with the enormous sadness caused by the disappearance of his parents, David Le Quesne argued before the magistrate. But because Roderick had made the mistake of committing further offences while on bail, he soon found himself languishing not at police headquarters but in Jersey's one prison, which is situated at La Moye, just a mile or so from his parents' bungalow at Clos de L'Atlantique.

Maureen Ellam applied to the prison authorities to visit Roderick there. 'By this stage I was thinking, did he . . . didn't he? I found that my suspicion would come and go in waves. But whatever he had or had not done, I reminded myself that he is my friends' child. And you don't ostracize him for what you think he might have done.'

Outraged that his application for bail had been refused, Roderick decided that he would protest most forcibly. Never one to do anything by half measures, he concluded that a hunger strike might well be the most effective method of registering his discontent. Writing from HM Prison, La Moye, he outlined his predicament to his aunt and uncle, the Clarks. He confided that a strong sense of having been treated unjustly by the legal process was the reason for his going on hunger strike. In the event, his concern for this action's effect on the Clarks, his grandmother and Mark, combined with the fear that his health would suffer a rapid decline, led him to abandon his protest after only four days. In any case, he admitted, in the end he was not strong enough to resist the food left in his cell by the warders. Nevertheless he maintained steadfastly that he had been morally right to make his grievance felt by refusing food, and added a poignant quotation emphasizing the individual's aloneness in the face of his or her knowledge of God. A postscript conceded that generally speaking prison life was not too bad: the food was good, and the other inmates and warders were interesting and most of them were kind.

It was at this time too that the police made another breakthrough. Police dog handlers found the remains of a bonfire close to the old family home at Grève de Lecq. In the debris were a number of personal items

117

belonging to the Newalls. It was clear that they had been transported from Clos de L' Atlantique for disposal. But not everything had been consumed by the flames. Fibres from a Bissell upholstery brush matching those from a carpet in the lounge were found. Other fibres matched a fawn carpet in the master bedroom, where Elizabeth Newall had lain bleeding. There was evidence of other items used in the clean-up operation, including fragments of a J cloth, of the kind found at the bungalow. The remains of Elizabeth's black handbag, one of those she purchased during a spending spree at Harrods the previous summer, were also recovered. So were a red Sheaffer pen, a compact and lipstick, a Givenchy perfume bottle and the charred remains of a cookery book. Nan Clark assisted the police in positively identifying all of these items as belonging to her sister. But most tellingly of all, both the bowl of Nicholas's pipe and the lenses of his glasses were also discovered among the ashes. Nicholas's prescription was so extremely rare that his optician assured the police that the lenses could only have belonged to the murdered man. Graham Nimmo was delighted with his find. It was a major development in the case.

The two sniffer dogs, Butch and Winston, on loan from the Lancashire police force, had come up trumps. It was clear that their experience in the reopened Moors Murders inquiry in the 1980s had served them well. But Detective Inspector Nimmo wanted them to deliver still more. If they could sniff out the Newalls' clothes, he reasoned, then they could sniff out their bodies too. He knew that the entire investigation was likely to falter unless the bodies were found. The black labrador and German shepherd dog therefore had to be kept happy. They were honoured guests indeed.

Graham Nimmo elaborates:

I had to beg, steal and borrow still-born piglets for those dogs, because dead pig meat has the nearest smell to humans. So twice a week, to keep the dogs in trim, we had to go and bury piglets on the sand dunes. I used to do this myself. They had no trouble at all in finding them. A kind local pig farmer helped us out. It was just as well that the public didn't see the dogs running around crazed with these dead piglets in their mouths. Then we would go off and give the piglets a proper burial afterwards.

It was certainly not for want of trying, for during their time on the island they were worked very hard indeed, but the Lancashire sniffer dogs never succeeded in uncovering the precise location of either Elizabeth or Nicholas Newall. One possible explanation was that the couple were not on the island at all. That was certainly Mark Newall's view, for he told the police that in his opinion his parents' bodies were likely to have been disposed of at sea.

Unlike others close to the Newall family, Angela Barnes never wavered in her conviction that

Roderick was deeply implicated in the disappearance of the friends she had helped to welcome to the Channel Islands twenty years earlier. Despite these suspicions Roderick was a regular visitor to her luxurious home. Apart from enjoying her company, he knew that Angela was a generous hostess who could always be relied upon to provide both cigarettes and alcohol.

'I had no doubt that he had bumped them off,' says Angela of the elder Newall son.

> So when he used to visit me I was apprehensive. I used to be careful what I said. One evening, though, I was feeling a bit braver. So I said to him: 'You know, there must have been three people who killed your parents' – because it was quite a big job. I reminded him that they were big people weighing at least twelve and fourteen stone. 'Oh no,' he said, 'that's easy, you can just carry them over your shoulder.' Not that he was admitting that he had done it, mind you. On another occasion he became quite emotional. He kept saying, 'I feel so sorry for Mark.' He repeated that same phrase at least three times. All the time I was trying to probe, to find out what exactly he was getting at. But again I couldn't get anything further from him.

Mark also had occasional contact with Angela. It was while Roderick was in prison serving his short sentence for the possession of cannabis that Mark telephoned from London. He was anxious for the wealthy heiress to ask Roderick to ring his brother on his number there as soon as possible.

'Will you please do that immediately?' he said.

Although somewhat taken back by Mark's tone, which made his request sound rather more like a command, Angela agreed that she would. After all, it was hardly a great deal to ask. Then Mark added a comment which Angela failed to understand, just as she had been unable to decipher Roderick's cryptic reference to Mark. The younger brother said to her, totally unprompted: 'You do realize, don't you, that I have absolute and complete control over my brother?'

Detective Inspector Nimmo knew that he too needed more control; and that in order to make progress with the investigation he had to interview both Roderick and Mark again. He negotiated a package with their lawyer, David Le Quesne, who was also their parents' legal representative. The agreement was that the boys would not be accused of anything at all. The purpose of speaking to them was merely to clarify a number of points. They were to be interviewed separately and Graham Nimmo further agreed that he would refrain from pointing out any discrepancies which might emerge in their answers. Otherwise, it was made clear, the brothers would insist on their advocate being present throughout and would have said nothing. Nimmo was prepared to proceed on this basis, on the grounds that something was likely to be better than nothing at all. The only

other policeman present at the interviews would be
Sergeant Adamson.

'It was a game,' Graham Nimmo admits.

A difficult one for me to play – and even more
difficult for them. When I came to interview the
second one, the first one did not know what the
other had said. And that was where we got a hell
of a lot of differences. These interviews went on
for several hours. They were asked such detailed
questions that they could not possibly have cobbled up their various answers together. Questions like: 'who dried up?, ' 'who washed up
after lunch?', 'who left something on the plate?',
'who did not?' And so on. They soon ran into
difficulty. But when they did so, they just
stopped speaking. It was difficult to remember
all the details, especially without notes. As soon
as you upset them they would say: 'Right, that's
it, I'm saying no more.' I would look at them.
And they would look at me. And then they
would say to me, eventually, 'Is that it now?'
They were totally arrogant and petulant. What
used to annoy me most was that they couldn't
bring themselves to say 'yes'. All they would say
was 'absolutely'. That became something of a
standing joke around the incident room. We
gleaned so much during these interviews that the
next morning Mark appeared and said that Roderick had been drunk. I said, 'Well, you brought
him in here at eight a.m. and he wasn't drunk

when he came in.' They had obviously patched up the story afterwards. That's why they asked for a copy of the tape. I thought that overall it had gone very well. And that we had sufficient evidence in order to be able to formally charge them.

Armed with this new information and backed up by an enormous amount of other detective work, Detective Inspector Nimmo set about compiling a comprehensive report on the case. He would urge his superiors, and through them the island's Attorney-General, Mr Philip Bailhache QC, to give the necessary consents so that both Roderick and Mark Newall could be prosecuted without further delay.

It was a frustrating time, but not just for the police officers involved. For those too who had been close to Elizabeth and Nicholas, the passage of one month after another with the case still unresolved was deeply upsetting. It was hardly surprising, then, that at various stages they all sought to vent their fury on the States of Jersey police force itself. 'It was just one big cock-up in the early days,' David Ellam insists. 'They just did too little too late. Why didn't they spot all that blood earlier on? Nimmo knew all about those boys. But they sat on him.'

It was a sentiment with which Nan Clark agreed, as her diary reveals:

Little or no interest by top police. Non existent during my visit. Adamson says he has difficulty persuading them to get time to continue, and is continually trying to justify time spent. Still no reply from police chief Parkinson to my letter. Went to Rouge Bouillon and couldn't get meeting with either Le Brocq or Le Breton. Maureen Ellam phoned. Said Le Breton had visited her. Told her to relax. Said there may never be a solution. Am beginning to despair.

So too was Assistant Chief Officer Bob Le Breton – so much so that he thought it would be a good idea if a senior officer could be brought over from the mainland to review the case. It was a courageous stance to take, and one which raised a few eyebrows at police headquarters at Rouge Bouillon. 'We saw that we were up against two highly intelligent lads,' he recalls. 'We knew that this case was a real stinker. No bodies – a crime scene and so on. So I put forward the idea of bringing in a reviewing officer. Because there is always some merit in an entirely fresh approach.'

In many respects Detective Chief Superintendent John Saunders, the head of Suffolk CID, was the ideal choice. Certainly his track record was most impressive: during 1987 alone he had headed no fewer than ten murder investigations, each one of which had resulted in arrests. But having spent several weeks going through the substantial amount of documentary and evidential material made available to him, he was unable to find fault with the manner in which the case had been conducted by the Jersey police. While he saw fit to make a number of minor recommendations, he sought to stress the point that they had done more than any force on the mainland would have done. 'If this case isn't cracked,' he noted, 'it certainly won't be through lack of effort.'

Shortly after his departure, however, it seemed that that effort might be paying off, for another piece of the complex Newall jigsaw appeared to have fallen into place. A shovel had been found during a cliff search at Noirmont. Inquiries soon revealed that it was part of a highly significant package of material. On the morning of Saturday 10 October 1987, the day of the Newalls' meal at the Sea Crest Hotel, a young man described as being of Aryan appearance had gone into Norman Ltd, a large hardware store situated by the docks in St Helier. There he had made a rather large and unusual purchase, the bill coming to £103.42, and paid for in cash. Taken separately, there was nothing remarkable about any of the items. But taken together they were of considerable interest to the police. For who else but a murderer seeking to dispose of one or more bodies, the police reasoned, would be interested in buying a saw, a pickaxe, knives, rope, shovels, lamps, plastic sacks, and two twelve-foot-square tarpaulins?

Just as he would pop in to visit Angela Barnes, so too would Roderick appear at Crow's Nest. He seemed to be particularly attached to his childhood home. And during the first six months after the murder of his parents, he would sometimes drop in on Maureen Ellam two or three times a week. It was as if he

125

needed to talk to someone, although during their many conversations they only ever talked around the subject. Eventually, tired of the shadow boxing and pretence, Maureen decided to confront Roderick directly. In doing so, however, she was choosing to forget that her husband had issued a ban of indefinite duration, strictly forbidding her to ever mention the murders while alone with Roderick at Crow's Nest. But by now Elizabeth Newall's friend was desperate to get to the heart of the matter, so she picked up the telephone and, blunt as always, left a terse message on an answering machine: 'I want to see one of you boys urgently today.'

Within half an hour Roderick had returned her call. Mark was attending to business in London. 'Well, I'm very busy today Mrs Ellam,' the elder brother replied. But when Maureen insisted that he make himself available, Roderick did so right away, and soon afterwards he arrived at Crow's Nest.

Although apprehensive at the prospect of challenging Roderick, Maureen was nevertheless impatient to begin. 'You have never asked me what I think happened to your parents,' she said.

Roderick ignored her remark, his eyes darting everywhere but towards those of his interrogator. Desperate to change the subject, he asked for some sugar in his coffee. Aware of what he was up to, Maureen continued undeterred. It was desperately important for her to say what she had to say, banning order or otherwise.

'I repeat. I said you have never asked me what I think might have happened to your parents.'

'Go on then,' Roderick replied rather gingerly, clearly feeling that he had been cornered.

'Right. Sit there. Shut up. Silence and listen.'

Together they went through to the sitting room, each clutching their coffee. The view was as spectacular as ever – on a clear day France can easily be seen – and Roderick had never tired of it during his many years at Crow's Nest. Like his father, he had been drawn towards sailing and the sea.

'I believe that there was a family fight that got out of hand.'

Roderick could not stop himself interrupting.

'Oh yes, Mrs Ellam, and there were so many of those.'

'I know, love. But please, I said no comment. I want silence.'

Then, aware of her vulnerability in the house, Maureen decided to concoct a version of events which she did not believe at all. It was merely a way of being able to broach the subject with Roderick. 'I believe that the withdrawn and ill-treated Mark flipped,' she said. 'And that you had to be there to help with the clear-up and everything else.'

Again Roderick tried to intervene.

'Mark is not as bad as you think he is, Mrs Ellam.'

By this stage the courage which had propelled Maureen to confront Roderick was beginning to peter out, and she was becoming increasingly distressed. But, struggling to keep her composure, she battled on.

'As I understand it, on this island under Norman law you will get forty years. I can't do that to you. If I thought that you would get five or ten years, I would say, "Come on, let's get it over with. Let's give them a decent burial." Goodness knows, living with it is going to be hard enough for you. And spending the rest of your life in prison is to no avail. So I don't know how to advise you. The only thing I can say to you is get the hell off of this island and never come back.'

The following day Roderick Newall left Jersey. It would be some time before he would set foot on the island again.

Graham Nimmo was reviewing the work carried out on the Newall case during the previous year. It was true that the bodies had not been found; he hardly needed reminding of that. But more than a thousand people had been interviewed; 350 statements taken; 1200 lines of inquiry pursued. These had certainly not all been in vain; far from it. For without them he would have been unable to complete the long and detailed report he was about to submit to his superiors. The detective was particularly pleased that he had been able to produce no fewer than forty separate reasons why both Roderick and Mark should be charged.

I was reporting to Martyn Le Brocq, the Chief Inspector. And then to Bob Le Breton, the Assistant Chief. Followed of course by the Chief himself. We had an important meeting together. I set out my various points before them. But it was considered just not to be enough. The Attorney-General agreed. This came as a complete and utter disappointment to me. I couldn't believe that he didn't accept what Jimmy Adamson and I had said. Then I thought back to what my father used to tell me. That once you put it on paper, if it goes to court, you give your evidence and that is the end of the matter. What happens to the guy doesn't matter in the slightest. But I have to admit that this refusal still hurt a lot.

Fifteen months after the murders, and with the inquiry now scaled down, Graham Nimmo could scarcely conceal his disappointment. It was the first murder case he had been unable to bring to a successful conclusion.

'Almost all avenues of inquiry have been exhausted,' he wrote to Nan Clark, in reply to one of her many letters designed to prod the police into further action.

The case remains open, however, and subject to continued investigation. While I appreciate your anxiety, I am unable to indicate if and when the case will be solved. But I know that you are aware of certain matters that were the subject of discussion between us on your earlier visit which have made the investigation very difficult to proceed.

Like his brother, Mark concluded that he was better off away from the island. In any event, his career as a fund manager meant he was darting between London, Paris and New York, and indeed all over the world. But unlike Roderick, who would talk about his parents from time to time, even if his remarks were sometimes a little obscure, Mark was silent on the subject. Even in the immediate aftermath of their disappearance, when a family friend had sought to express shock and sorrow, Mark had chosen to ignore the remark. Always a remote and lonely figure, he appeared to withdraw even more into his shell. His former friend and jogging partner, Nicholas Symonds, recalls:

> I only saw Mark once after the disappearance, when he came into my car showrooms. We had already drifted apart because I was getting married. Even so he was extremely distant. I knew that we couldn't talk about what had happened. But just the same it was almost as if a different person had walked in.

Mark was rather more relaxed when in Paris. Living in a stylish apartment in the Rue Paul Valéry, in the select sixteenth *arrondissement*, he threw all of his time, energy and considerable talent into his job with the Banque Arabe et Internationale d'Investissement, where he was responsible for managing monies referred to as the 'Rainbow Fund'. Always travelling Club Class and with no expense spared on his own wardrobe, he would stay in the very best hotels, money apparently no object. All in all, it was not a bad life.

The *Jersey Evening Post* never allowed the Newall case to slip from its headlines, even though very often there was nothing of substance to report. 'The Newalls: Two years on and still no solution,' the paper announced. The case remained an unsolved mystery, spawning numerous articles and two separate television documentaries. Even *Bergerac* star John Nettles temporarily became a real-life sleuth in an attempt to solve the case, carrying out a number of inquiries of his own. 'Critics have accused the series' storylines of being too far-fetched,' he admitted, but added: 'Yet they do not even begin to compare with this case.'

But not even Bergerac could crack the Newall case. It seemed that nobody could. Thus, while the file was not closed, officers and detectives were assigned to other duties. The cost of the investigation had already been vast and a balance had to be struck between the expenditure of public funds on the one hand and the likelihood of a successful resolution of the case on the other. In the event the scales came down firmly on the side of inaction. Unless and until new evidence was forthcoming, there was nothing more that the Jersey force could do. For Graham Nimmo in particular, it was a bitter pill to swallow:

This case affected me. Eventually I came out of the police force on a sick pension with stress and hypertension. It was on New Year's eve 1989–90 that I suddenly felt my heart beating in my arms and legs. The doctor took my blood pressure and said: 'Right – that's it, you're going home.' It was absolutely sky high. It wasn't that the Newall case got to me; rather a combination of things. I had a young detective constable, twenty-two years old, a cracking lad, the ex-chief officer's son. And he died in tragic circumstances. I had to investigate that death too. So it was a combination of things of which the Newall case was part. I think it was all the murders I had dealt with over the years, all the dead bodies that I had looked at – it must have built up within me. I spent a lot of time talking to a psychologist, with whom I shed many a tear. Because for the first time it all came out. You suddenly realize that working a sixteen- or seventeen-hour day for eight to ten years gets to you. I had had no contact with my two boys. They had both left home and gone off to university. Where had all the years gone? I was told that I had to change my lifestyle. I knew that I couldn't go back, because my old habits would have crept back in. That's the way I am. But it broke my bloody heart to come out of the police in that way. It wasn't what I had had in mind.

Roderick Newall, however, seemed to be having the time of his life. He was sailing the family yacht, *Chanson de Lecq*, from one part of the world to another. 'Roderick phoned at 11 a.m. from Tangiers,' Nan Clark noted in her diary. 'Says he may go on to Casa Blanca. Hurricanes still preventing him crossing Atlantic and winds not good for Spain.'

Within a few months he had made his way to the Caribbean. New Zealand and South America were also on his itinerary. Delighted to have left the Army, he was doing what he had always wanted to do: leading the life of a gentleman and sailing the high seas. He also appeared to be living it up, as his aunt's diary reveals: 'Roderick phoned mother from Barbados. Gay (Newall) phoned. Said Roderick living very expensively in Barbados. Leaves for Venezuela tomorrow.'

It was a life of excitement and adventure. Next stop, the Falkland Islands. There Roderick managed to find a job on a trawler, the *Forest*, which travelled between the Falklands and Chile on a regular basis as a supply ship. He soon proved himself to be a lively worker, and popular on deck. But the Captain, George Betts, could not understand his reluctance to supply the name and address of his next of kin, an absolute imperative for insurance purposes. It was only several months later, when Captain Betts happened to catch sight of a press cutting on the Newall case, that he realized why.

Roderick enjoyed great popularity among the Falkland Islanders too. And, as always, he was very popular with the girls. Sandy Emandas remembers him well:

I knew Rod for two years. We became close friends. He was very gregarious, friendly, full of life, always wanting to chat to people, interesting and interested. Rod told me about the case, although we didn't talk about it much. He was very well-liked out here, always wanting to take people out sailing with him.

Nor had his sporting prowess deserted him. He once turned up in his yacht at Pebble Island, just north-west of Falkland Sound, where a tournament was taking place in which a medal was on offer to the winner of a one-mile cross-country run. The former officer had not prepared for it at all. Undeterred, he took off his jacket, rolled up his trouser legs and surprised everybody by winning the race handsomely, beating the previous champion and a number of other excellent runners in the process. As the years went by, he appeared to be increasingly settled in the Falklands. The remote islands in the South Atlantic seemed to have become home. He was invited to give away a girl at a wedding, established a chartering business with a Frenchman, and befriended a man by the name of Jérôme Poncet, an explorer who owned Beaver Island, and who spent a good deal of his time travelling around the Antarctic on his yacht *Damion*. One day Roderick hoped that he would be able to do likewise. Whatever the outcome of his various business projects, for Roderick Newall it was a healthy, outdoor life which suited him well, as was revealed by one of a number of letters he sent to his aunt. In this he wrote enthusiastically of the people he had met in a part of the world not yet overrun by tourists. In passing he referred to an estrangement between Uncle Stephen and Mark, about which he seemed to be rather in the dark. He confided too that there were many questions about his father that he now regretted never having asked, either through lack of time or inclination.

He might well have left Jersey behind. And, apparently, the mystery of the murder of his parents. But his hot-headed temperament went with him everywhere, however remote the location. Just as he had been involved in fights at Radley, so was he unable to restrain himself in the Falklands from setting about a female New Zealander during an argument between them. Fists flying, he assaulted the young woman so badly that she was hospitalized, although no criminal prosecution followed. Nevertheless Roderick was known to Kenneth Greenland, Chief Constable in the Falkland Islands police, whose officers occasionally kept tabs on his movements, especially when he was in the Port Stanley area. For despite the huge distance between them, Jersey and the Falkland Islands are alike in that in both places rumour and gossip spread fast. Not surprisingly, therefore, when it came to the Newall case, it was not long before the Falklanders' tongues began to wag in earnest.

With Mark often travelling from one country or continent to another, and with Roderick now based in the Falklands, communication between the brothers was not easy to maintain. Yet both were acutely aware of the importance of keeping in touch. Every now and then, therefore, relatives were called upon to assist in this process. Not that their method of communication was conventional, as Nan Clark's diary reveals: 'R back in Falklands. Has asked that M contact him at public phone box at a given time. Mother passed on message.'

In January 1991, a little over three and a half years since they were last seen together in public, Elizabeth and Nicholas Newall were officially presumed dead. An application had been made by David Le Quesne to Jersey's Royal Court under Article 8 of the island's 1949 Probate Law. It did not take too long to persuade the Bailiff, Sir Peter Crill, to declare them dead, for the evidence of their demise was overwhelming. The Home

Office forensic expert, Dr David Northcott, was called in to remind the court of the bloodbath which had taken place at Clos de L'Atlantique during the autumn of 1987. Even the police were there to testify that the presumption of death was an entirely legitimate conclusion. Their only regret was that they had been unable to apprehend those guilty of the murders. And then Mark Newall flew in from London, and checked in at the four-star L'Horizon at St Brelade. He told the court that the chances were that both his parents were dead. Indeed, this had been his view for some time.

> I believe this for three reasons. I have not seen or heard from them for more than three years. I have seen no evidence that they have used any of their financial assets in those three years, and also largely because of information given to me by the police. They have indicated that they are investigating murder.

Mark had put his case well. The following day the *Jersey Evening Post* reported the Royal Court's ruling: 'The Newall estate: brothers inherit everything.' In fact, the Bailiff was merely implementing what both Elizabeth and Nicholas had stipulated in their wills.

'That's it then,' Maureen Ellam declared in the summer of 1992, aware that the fifth anniversary of the disappearance of her friends was not so far away.

> It's all over. The awful thing is though that I know that they are buried on this island, and I would

think not very far from me. It's so frustrating to be so near and yet so far. They should be given a decent burial. There should be somewhere where I can go and pick some of those lovely flowers which Elizabeth planted at Crow's Nest and take to her grave. So I will never forget them. Their relatives and friends who loved them will never forget them. For the murderers though it's all over. They're home and dry.

Just a few miles away Angela Barnes picked up her telephone and dialled 69996, the number of the police headquarters at Rouge Bouillon. At the main switchboard she asked to speak to Jimmy Adamson. She had acquired some new information which she thought might be of considerable interest to him. Nor had she forgotten her friends.

7

Taped

He had planned it as a special birthday treat. Stephen Newall, Nicholas's twin, and his wife had travelled across Scotland from their home in Dumbarton to the Dunkeld House Resort Hotel in Perthshire. Set in almost three hundred acres of grounds and boasting its own two-mile stretch of the River Tay, renowned for its salmon and trout, it was a most agreeable hotel, and an ideal base for exploring the Highlands. Stephen Newall was determined to make his wife Gay's sixtieth birthday a truly memorable occasion.

It was at that time too, towards the middle of July 1992, that Nan Clark received a telephone call at her London home. It was Roderick. Assuming that it was a long-distance call, she asked her nephew if he was phoning from the South Atlantic. No he replied, he was in Fulham, not far from her own London home.

Although she was a little taken aback to hear Roderick, Nan was delighted that he had got in touch, and immediately invited him for dinner that evening. It had been at least three years since they had seen each other.

When Roderick arrived at the Clarks' house in Hurlingham Square he was brimming with enthusiasm about his latest project. He looked fit and healthy, despite having lost a little weight. Sitting near to a large portrait of his mother Elizabeth, painted when she was eighteen, he reported that he had managed to sell the family yacht, *Chanson de Lecq*, and had put the proceeds towards the purchase of the sixty-six-foot *Austral Soma*. He had been looking for a suitable vessel for some time and was convinced that he had found it. Although almost ten years old, the yacht had every imaginable modern appliance. And Roderick already had plans of his own to install a central-heating system run off an Aga-style stove, an eminently sensible idea since together with his crew he was likely to be sailing to and from the Antarctic. The *Austral Soma* was the boat which was going to form the basis of his business once he had brought it back to the Falklands. Everything was in place. Mark had also seen it and been likewise impressed. Although lacking his younger brother's flair for finance, Roderick nevertheless appeared to have been rather efficient, and proudly produced an illustrated brochure for his aunt to inspect. This provided a most engaging description of South Atlantic charter excursions aboard the yacht.

After a couple of gin and tonics the Clarks and their nephew sat down to eat. But Alister, a doctor, was to be deprived of dinner that Saturday evening, for he was called out to attend to a patient, leaving Roderick alone with his aunt. Not that they found themselves short of conversation. Roderick could hardly deliver his news quickly enough, punctuating it with his views on Greenpeace, the ozone layer, the Galápagos Islands, drug addiction and other topical issues. Naturally he had never said so while at Radley or in the Army, but his view remained that the taking of drugs could have a positive role to play in enabling people to develop a deeper and fuller perspective in life, a contention with which his aunt soon took issue. Whatever the other arguments for incarceration, it was clear that his short spell at HM Prison La Moye had not sent him back into the world full of contrition. Nor was it the case that Roderick's own experience with drugs had always been so deep or meaningful, for he freely admitted that he had once burnt all his clothes after a particularly bad drug experience.

Next on the agenda was the subject of mediums, Nan Clark reporting that one had once sent her a message from Elizabeth, albeit via a friend. Always receptive to new experiences, Roderick asked if his mother had ever appeared to her.

'Yes,' his aunt replied, 'the night she died.'

He did not pause to ask precisely which night that was. It was not the date but the content which was of interest to him.

'And what did she say?'

Nan Clark described the very vivid nightmare she had had in which she dreamed of Elizabeth's death.

141

She told of how, during the nightmare, her sister had said: 'I told you he meant it when he said that he would kill me, I told you it would happen – but leave the matter rest.'

Roderick was fascinated. He had always had an interest in the supernatural. But Elizabeth's command was one with which Nan Clark had been unwilling to comply. For how could the process of mourning be experienced properly while the murders remained shrouded in mystery?

'So, despite what she said, I would still like to know what happened,' Roderick's aunt said.

'Even if you knew exactly what happened,' he replied, 'you would still not understand.'

What exactly was her nephew saying? The implication was surely that he knew something which his aunt did not. If so, what? Was he perhaps admitting that he might have had a role to play in her death? Whatever the case, it was imperative to draw him out more. Not in order to promptly pass on to the police any information which might emerge, but merely because Nan Clark felt that the truth had eluded her for far too long.

'Why wouldn't I understand?' she asked. 'Try me.'

'Because I don't understand myself.'

Sensing that Roderick was unlikely to reveal any more, his aunt allowed the conversation to move on, although hardly to an entirely new subject. She was equally anxious to find out where the bodies might be buried – an issue more important to her than any admission of guilt or other explanation. For without the recovery of Elizabeth and Nicholas's bodies, there could never be a decent, dignified funeral. And she had found it an extremely precarious existence having to live with her grief on hold. She therefore described to her nephew how helicopters had been used in the searches in Jersey, aware that Roderick might well have something useful to add.

'Any ideas?' she asked.

This time, silence. Having already said more than might have been in his best interests, Roderick chose, uncharacteristically, to hold his tongue. Or was it simply because he genuinely had nothing to say on the matter? At half past midnight, and with Alister having returned, Roderick said goodbye to his aunt and uncle, adding that he was hoping to be able to travel up to Scotland in due course to visit relatives, before setting off once again for the high seas.

At no stage did it occur to Nan Clark that she and Roderick had had a conversation which might be of interest to the police. It was not that she was trying to protect her nephew in any way; rather that she had all but given up on the Jersey police, having tired of constantly trying to coax and cajole them into action. In any event, it had been made very clear to her that as far as the police case was concerned, the Newall investigation had virtually ground to a halt. It was a lesson which Detective Inspector Nimmo had learned some time before. The assumption that the inquiry was closed was thus not an unreasonable one. After all, it had been almost five years since Elizabeth and Nicholas had first been reported missing.

Angela Barnes showed no such reticence. As soon as

Nan Clark had given her an account of what had happened during their meeting in London – for the two women were regularly in touch by phone – she knew that there were certain people at Rouge Bouillon who would be very interested indeed. And most especially Jimmy Adamson, recently promoted to Detective Inspector. The Newall case had never once begun to fade from his mind, whatever the official status of the investigation. He had maintained contact with all the key players: Stephen Newall in Scotland, Nan Clark, both in London and Spain, and Maureen Ellam and Angela Barnes in Jersey. So when Angela telephoned him, it came as no great surprise, merely one of a series of updates on the case. What she told him, though, sent him dashing upstairs to his bosses on the top floor. It was difficult to be sure, but if he had understood Angela correctly, it seemed that Roderick might well be preparing to confess – if he had not done so already.

Adamson knocked on the door of Detective Superintendent Paul Marks, the new head of Jersey's CID, and therefore nominally in charge of the Newall case. Informing him of what had been said in London, he added that Roderick Newall was apparently on his way up to Scotland to meet his uncle and aunt.

'The decision to go for it was immediate,' Paul Marks recalls.

But I knew that there was no point in going to Scotland unless the Scottish Regional Crime Squad was going to co-operate fully with us. We obviously couldn't take all the technical resources up there with us and we naturally wanted to record anything going to be said. Nor did we know if Stephen Newall would work with us, although Jimmy felt sure that he would. I told Jimmy what I had in mind and instructed him to find Stephen Newall, to seek his co-operation.

The last time Stephen Newall had set eyes on Roderick was at the cremation of Kenneth Newall in Guernsey, some seven weeks after the disappearance of Elizabeth and Nicholas. It had not been the ideal moment, but he had taken advantage of the occasion to reprove both his nephews for their failure to co-operate with the police. He had always gone out of his way to help the police with their inquiries; it would have been unthinkable to have done otherwise. Not surprisingly, therefore, his relationship with both Roderick and Mark had been strained ever since.

For a person for whom policing was a second choice, Paul Marks, Jersey born and bred, had risen through the island's force very rapidly indeed, reaching the rank of Inspector by the age of thirty. He had, however, nurtured quite different ambitions at one time.

I wanted to be an artist actually. I had a reasonable portfolio; I could paint and had been accepted by an art college. My heart was in art – I would sometimes paint until three or four in the morning. But at the same time I was a realist. So I joined the force from school as a cadet for eighteen months, after which I went to England for basic training as a constable. I was proud to wear the uniform, although there were quite a lot of sloppy practices in those days. Walking the beat at the age of eighteen you certainly learn about human nature, especially its darker side. I particularly enjoyed my work with the Special Branch, of which I eventually became head, because that brought me into contact with the intelligence world. That was both challenging and stimulating. That kind of training teaches you not to go for the obvious, to keep an open mind. That values aren't simply black and white. And that's been my approach to policing ever since.

Before making his final decision on when to go to Scotland, Paul Marks had prepared a lengthy fax for the Scottish Regional Crime Squad, sending it through to Chief Constable level, in which he formally requested their assistance. He knew precisely what was required. It was clearly going to be a major and enormously costly operation, involving sophisticated surveillance techniques and other electronic equipment, technical resources and personnel, and plenty of back-up for security. After all, they were dealing with a potential murderer. It was to be so substantial an operation, in fact, that it would have been impossible for the Jersey police to have mounted it unaided. The island's force was simply too small. But aware of their own limitations, they had undergone thorough training and so knew what to ask for and how to go about getting it. The Scottish police rang back right away to say that all the necessary consents had been granted. They were on stand-by, waiting to be told precisely where and when. As it turned out, it was some ten hours before the Scots could be told what they needed to know, and this involved more than mere details.

Adamson had not yet been able to make contact with Stephen Newall, the key to the entire operation. He was neither at home nor at his company's offices in Helensburgh. Then, finally, his personal secretary disclosed to a visiting Crime Squad officer that he was in Perthshire with his wife, spending a few days at the Dunkeld House Resort Hotel. This meant that the police work which Detective Superintendent Marks and Detective Inspector Adamson had assumed would take place in Rhu, in the west of Scotland, would now have to be transferred elsewhere and the necessary consents applied for.

Stephen Newall knew that his nephew was looking for him, because Nan Clark had telephoned to say that Roderick was heading for Scotland. So when Stephen received Adamson's call it was immediately assumed that he would continue to co-operate with the inquiry. But this was a very difficult position for him. He wanted to help the police, and that had been his attitude all along. The case concerned not only the murder of his twin brother but his sister-in-law too. And he longed for the day when the whole ghastly affair would come to a close. At the same time he was not eager to be seen to be attempting to ensnare or entrap his nephew in any way. And what if Roderick was entirely innocent? How would he justify his actions afterwards? First Jimmy Adamson telephoned him, and then Paul Marks did likewise. They both put pressure on him, urging him to go along with the police plan. They were convinced that it would be their last opportunity to crack the case, if it was ever going to be cracked at all. Taking the moral high ground, they reminded the boys' uncle that it was his duty. After a while he appeared to change tack slightly. What exactly would be required of him? Once they started discussing the details of the operation, Marks and Adamson knew that Stephen Newall's support was likely to be forthcoming after all, just as Adamson had predicted from the outset. The trick was to put everything in place quickly and professionally so that Stephen and Gay would find it difficult to pull out of the operation.

Aware of the issue of the admissibility of any tape recording in future court proceedings, Paul Marks briefed Stephen Newall on how he ought to conduct himself during the meeting. He was at pains to point out that it was vitally important not to lead Roderick in any way. Any admission had to flow freely and naturally from him. It had to be entirely voluntary – not a response to questions which might give the impression of having been carried out on behalf of the police. It was an extremely delicate balance to strike.

'And what if he says nothing?' Roderick's uncle asked. 'Can I ask questions myself?'

Aware that Roderick was first visiting his grandmother, Granny Nelson, at her home in North Berwick, Stephen rang him there. Roderick was pleased because, like the police, he had been having difficulty making contact with his uncle and aunt. The best thing to do, Stephen suggested, was to meet up at the Dunkeld House Resort Hotel. And he gave the number of his suite, room 138. They agreed to meet at three o'clock. Bidding farewell to his grandmother, Roderick set off by car for Edinburgh, crossed the Forth Bridge, and settled down for the drive to Dunkeld.

Meanwhile, Paul Marks, the policeman supposed to be in overall charge of the operation, was stranded at London's Heathrow airport with Jimmy Adamson. Once they had been sure that the operation was on, they grabbed their overnight bags and left for the airport. They had five hours to get to Perthshire for the three p.m. meeting and could afford no delays. However, they had just failed to make the Edinburgh flight, and had to fly to Glasgow instead. In addition to arranging for a hire car to be ready for collection on their arrival in Scotland, Marks was almost continuously making or receiving calls on his mobile phone. With it he was able to liaise with the Scottish police; without it the operation might well have floundered.

Paul Marks recalls the thoughts that went through his mind as they drove through Scotland:

Luckily I had my licence with me. I drove and Jimmy did the rally co-driver bit, mapping us there. We drove fast. Because the plane only left at eleven-thirty and we had to be in deepest Perthshire by three p.m., when Roderick was due to arrive. It was exciting; a kind of battle of wits in which you are constantly trying to put yourself in the mind of the potential killer. We knew that we had set up something special, and that the Scottish Regional Crime Squad had diverted huge resources for us. They hadn't had much time either. There was great pressure all round. Had all the technical gear arrived in time? Was the room secure? Were the rooms properly linked? All that was being done by other people – so in a sense we were rather out of control.

The two Jersey policemen were making good progress, at times speeding along at well over eighty miles per hour, even though they had no dispensation to do so in Scotland and were unfamiliar with the roads. Then Jimmy Adamson got through on the mobile phone to Chief Inspector Jim Smith, the surveillance team commander from the Scottish Squad. The Jersey policemen were seeking advice on a place where they could stop before the hotel. They agreed on a roundabout near Dunkeld. Suddenly disaster threatened: roadworks. There was nothing they could do but sit it out. Valuable time was slipping away. But then, as the traffic flowed again, Detective Superintendent Marks did his best to make up for lost time, and before long they were approaching the outskirts of Dunkeld.

What Paul Marks did not know was that Roderick happened to be approaching the same roundabout. It was as well therefore that their suspect, driving an F-registered black VW Golf GTi, was already being monitored by the Scottish surveillance team. The

A patrol from the Royal Navy frigate HMS *Argonaut* about to board Roderick's yacht the *Austral Soma* shortly after his dramatic arrest on the high seas for murder (*Press Association*)

The *Austral Soma* is escorted into Gibraltar by HMS *Ranger* (*Press Association*)

Police officers who worked on the Newall murder case:
top: Detective Inspector Graham Nimmo; *right*: Assistant Chief Officer Paul Marks (*Jersey Evening Post*), deep in thought at the time of the search for the bodies of Elizabeth and Nicholas Newall; *left, top*:Detective Inspector James Adamson; *centre*: Detective Inspector Martin Fitzgerald; *bottom*: Detective Sergeant Charles MacDowall (*States of Jersey Police*)

Roderick leaves Gibraltar's Moorish Castle Prison ...(*Mail Newspapers plc*)

...and arrives in Jersey handcuffed to Detective Inspector Martin Fitzgerald with Assistant Chief Officer Paul Marks, right. David Le Quesne, the Newall family's lawyer, can be seen dismbarking from the aircraft (*Channel Island Picture Agency*)

Mark Newall's work often took him overseas; he always travelled club class (*Mail Newspaper plc*)

Mark in handcuffs on the way to court in St Helier (*Channel Island Picture Agency*)

Chinese rice-flails, similar to those used to kill Elizabeth and Nicholas Newall (*Times Newspapers Limited*)

Home Office pathologist Gyan Fernando examines remains watched by Jersey's public health pathologist Greg Monteith (*Jersey Evening Post*)

Roderick was given permission to leave Jersey's La Moye prison for a few hours in order to assist the police in the search for his parents. Here he can be seen running away from the press corps, handcuffed to a detective (*Jersey Evening Post*)

An army friend of Roderick digging a trench, almost identical to the one found at Greve de Lecq

Grève de lecq, where the Newall boys lived as children and where they were later to bury the bodies of their parents. Roderick used to visit Maureen Ellam, the current owner of their old house, in order to inspect his parents' graves, although he did not, of course, announce that fact (*top: Reg C. Queree*)

Roderick (left) and Mark at Jersey's Royal Court on 8 August 1994 when they were given two concurrent life sentences and six years' imprisonment respectively (*Jersey Evening Post*)

vehicle belonged to Emma-Jane Lonsdale, a portrait painter and friend of a friend, who had lent Roderick both her car and her flat during her absence in Italy. The Scottish police advised their colleagues from Jersey to pull in for a few minutes, and wait by the gates of a brewery just a few hundred yards before the roundabout.

Almost immediately a guard from the brewery appeared. He wanted to know what the two men, neither of them a lightweight, were up to.

'We are police officers from Jersey,' Paul Marks said by way of explanation.

The security guard had heard many a tall story in his time. But this one, he thought, took some beating. Without further ado, he dialled 999, convinced that the brewery was about to be robbed, and not for the first time either. Within a few minutes Chief Inspector Jim Smith appeared on the scene, and promptly flashed a warrant card at the guard, confirming that what he had been told was the truth. With the security guard still struggling to understand why two plain-clothes police-men from Jersey should be sitting in an unmarked vehicle outside a brewery in Scotland, Marks and Adamson transferred into the Chief Inspector's car, from where they were able to maintain radio contact with the entire team. Everything was in place.

The constant danger was that Roderick would realize that he was being followed. Or that he would recognize Jimmy Adamson, whom he had known since the earli-est days of the investigation. They had spent many an hour together at Rouge Bouillon. The problem was resolved by inviting the Detective Inspector to lower his head and lay down in the back of the car. Never one to shirk his duty, Adamson obliged.

Paul Marks remembers:

So Jimmy had this wonderful view of the carpet as we approached the country hotel. Then, just as Roderick was turning into the drive, he suddenly stopped. We all thought that the surveillance had been blown out, because he was military, and therefore trained in surveillance techniques. Not so. He had simply stopped to change his shirt before meeting his uncle and aunt.

Suitably spruced up, but a little apprehensive about the impending reunion, Roderick entered the hotel. What he did not know was that a few moments after his arrival, two officers from the States of Jersey police were doing likewise, albeit through the rear doors. Together they made their way to the first floor, and crept along the wooden-floored corridor past the bugged suite. Aware that if Roderick chose to walk out at that moment the operation would come to an abrupt end, they were very tense. Then, two or three doors away, the two policemen went into the room that had been set aside for them. It was full of police personnel, and it was clear that it had been set up in a very professional manner. It was hardly possible to move because of the amount of electronic surveillance equipment that had been installed in the room: there were cables, wires, aerials and tape everywhere.

'Put those on,' Marks said to Adamson, pointing to a set of headphones, 'and don't take them off.' Settling himself into a corner of the room, Adamson began to log the key events taking place in room 138 – standard crime-squad practice in such cases. A broadcast-quality tape recorder had been hidden underneath one of the chairs in the Newalls' suite and its three-hour tape had already begun to turn.

The conversation began innocently enough, with a discussion about the then Duke of Atholl, who had initiated the building of Dunkeld House one year before the turn of the century. But Roderick's passion was the sea and he reeled off an impressive list of the places he had visited: the Cook Islands, New Zealand, Australia, the Falkland Islands – and many more besides. Proud of his project with the *Austral Soma*, he produced the brochure for his aunt and uncle to peruse, just as he had done three days earlier in London for Nan Clark. Stephen and Gay Newall made all the right noises. However, with other, far more serious, matters weighing on their minds, they struggled to summon up the enthusiasm which Roderick's globetrotting would otherwise have warranted.

To those listening in, it sounded like an ordinary conversation between a nephew visiting his aunt and uncle. It seemed so ordinary, in fact, that after some forty minutes a number of the Scottish officers were beginning to wonder what it was all about. So was Paul Marks. He could not help noticing that occasionally looks were being exchanged among his Scottish colleagues, as if to imply that they had been misled. For so far the dialogue hardly sounded like the stuff of which murder inquiries or confessions are made. Sticking resolutely to his brief, the Newall brothers' uncle had so far resisted the temptation to ask a single leading or awkward question.

Of Stephen Newall's role, Paul Marks says:

> I had suggested to Stephen that there might be an opportunity at teatime to pop the question about Nan's call. I thought that Roderick's training would not allow him to just walk out on his uncle and aunt. I also went to public school, my father was also a teacher – and I figured that he would behave with good manners at all times, even if he was confronted with a difficult question.

Tea duly served, Stephen Newall knew that the time had come for him to turn the conversation towards what had hitherto been unmentionable.

'I had a rather strange phone call from Aunt Nan,' he said to his nephew.

'What I said to Nan,' Roderick replied, 'was that I still had no idea why it happened or what caused it.'

It was exactly as Nan had reported, but at this time with the difference that what Roderick said was being captured on tape. Adding that there was no way to bring his parents back, Roderick said that he had come to live with that fact. But there could be no stopping him now. He had always feared meeting Stephen; he was afraid that he would be unable to maintain his silence, to prevent himself from spilling out the truth.

For as he looked into the eyes of his uncle, Nicholas Newall's identical twin, how could he have come any closer to looking into those of his own father?

Not that Roderick had any intention of languishing in prison for twenty-five years, for he announced to his uncle and aunt that if the police moved in on him he had a suicide plan. Apart from anything else, he added, the stigma was likely to hasten the demise of Granny Nelson. He carried the blame for this crime. Nor were there any mitigating circumstances.

A little farther along the darkened corridor, the ears of those same Scottish officers who had earlier appeared more than a little bored by the operation were pricking up. No more strange glances now. Everybody was listening intently.

'You could have cut the air with a knife,' Paul Marks would later recall. 'There was so much tension in that room, it was so emotionally charged. I was only tuning in from time to time, but it was clear that everybody was absolutely riveted by the conversation.'

Like Nan Clark, Stephen Newall was desperately anxious to find out where the bodies were located. 'I don't suppose there would be much evidence of the bodies now,' he ventured, deliberately vague. Roderick soon put his uncle right. His parents' bodies were wrapped up in plastic and camouflaged. Not only that, they would have certain clothing on which would, as he put it, 'pin it down to the night'. What Roderick was saying was what the Jersey police had suspected all along: the only clothes of the Newalls' never to have been found were those which they had worn to dinner at the Sea Crest Hotel on the evening of Saturday 10 October 1987. In other words, they were the clothes in which Elizabeth and Nicholas had gone to their final resting-place that night.

'All the time I was considering what to do with this information,' Paul Marks explains.

> I had no power in Scotland. I wanted an opinion as to whether there was enough to arrest him there and then. I thought that there was. But sometimes it was difficult to hear what was being said, because the tape recorder was picking up every-thing – from the fridge switching itself on and off to low-flying military aircraft outside. There was also the problem of whether the tape recorded in the room had worked, as that was the only one which could be used in evidence. It was my job to make sure we got it right. I wanted to hear more.

And there was more to come. For Roderick then volunteered the information that he was forced to live with his guilt. If he had been a Catholic, he said, he would be seeking absolution. In fact he was quite looking forward to seeing his parents 'on the far side'.

'To say you are sorry?' Stephen Newall asked.

'No.'

While he was aware that he was in urgent need of legal advice, Roderick nevertheless seemed indifferent to the consequences of the situation, saying: 'I don't think I'd mind too much paying the price.'

Whatever the final outcome, Stephen replied, he

hoped and prayed that his nephew would find some way of leading the authorities to the bodies, wherever they might be.

'I've got the greatest admiration for the way that Stephen and Gay conducted themselves,' Paul Marks says, adding that:

Stephen was somehow able to remain in control of his emotions. Of course he was aware that the tape was running, but the power of the occasion overtook both of them. In fact it almost overtook us all. And he refrained from asking other questions to which he wanted to have answers. Questions like: 'What did you do to them?', 'how did it happen?' and most especially, 'did they suffer?'

Four hours had passed. There had even been a break in the proceedings, during which time Roderick and his uncle walked in the grounds of the hotel and a second three-hour tape was hurriedly loaded. But the time had come for Roderick to leave. Just before he was about to go, his aunt thanked him for the birthday gift of handkerchiefs which he had presented to her on his arrival. 'I'm sorry about the other present,' he added, almost as an aside. And with those words he made ready to leave.

'Naturally I was pleased with what we had heard,' Paul Marks remembers.

I felt as if I had been there in the room with them. But I was very concerned about everyone's safety.

I also wanted Jimmy's opinion on if he thought that we had enough to convict. 'Not without the bodies,' he said. That put some doubt in my mind. Plus I had been told by Jim Smith, who was heading up the Scottish side of the operation, that if we were to arrest Roderick without a warrant, then they would only have been able to hold him for six hours. I asked him what he would do in such circumstances. And he said: 'Don't take him here.' Then I phoned the Attorney-General in Jersey. He wanted to hear the tape for himself. I wasn't particularly worried, though, because I knew that we had five surveillance cars working with us, so that I had at least some time to work out what to do. At one stage I said that one of our options was to take him at the gate. This was heard over the covert radio sets, and they were about to pounce on him. I said: 'No, no, no' – it was just a thought. Whereupon Roderick drove off. I said: 'Right, stay with him.'

Stephen and Gay Newall had carried out their roles with the greatest of dignity and courage. The topic of conversation could hardly have been more horrific: murder in the family. There had been talk of bodies and burials, of the violent death of loved ones. And yet for the most part they had managed to keep their feelings in check. As soon as Roderick had left their suite, however, that control abruptly ceased. They were both completely overcome, devastated by what they had heard. Jersey's Attorney-General would come to his own conclusions in due course. So too would the police. But Stephen and Gay knew very well that they had just heard their twenty-six-year-old nephew, Roderick Innes Nelson Newall, whose arrival into the world they could remember only too clearly, admitting that he was responsible for the murder of his parents. Not matricide or patricide, but both. The tape recorder still turning, capturing their grief, the couple were left alone for a while. It had certainly been a most memorable occasion; though hardly the birthday treat Stephen Newall had had in mind.

He had been fined for speeding just six weeks earlier, but clearly it had not deterred him at all. For Roderick began to drive at extremely high speeds, up to a hundred and ten miles per hour at times. Making for Edinburgh on the A9, he soon began a progress which seemed most odd, stopping on the hard shoulder once or twice, doubling back on himself from time to time, and frequently popping in and out of service stations, each time making several calls from pay phones. And yet it was not odd at all. Having realized that he was being followed, he was doing his best to give those pursuing him the slip. Well acquainted with surveillance, the former army officer had soon noted down in his Filofax the registration number of one of the unmarked police vehicles from the Scottish Crime Squad. They should not have been spotted, but as the light began to fade and the traffic thinned, it must have been ever more obvious to Roderick, from the constant glare of fast-moving lights behind him, that his every manoeuvre was being shadowed.

Then, a little after midnight, just as the Scottish team were preparing to hand over to their counterparts in England, Roderick put his foot right down, and his Golf GTi disappeared into the night. He was last sighted at a double roundabout by Junction 21 on the A57, and a search was carried out for two hours. But he was gone.

'I knew that the team had been working for me for twenty hours and I owed them everything for reopening the case, Paul Marks recalls. 'I just said: "OK, that's fine." '

In fact it was not fine at all.

8

'Boy, Have We Got A Surprise For You'

At approximately two o'clock on the afternoon of Wednesday 15 July 1992, the telephone rang at the Clarks' home in Hurlingham Square. It was Roderick, calling from France. He announced that he had been followed by the police after leaving the Dunkeld House Resort Hotel. Each time he had stopped at a motorway service station to ring his aunt and uncle, the same vehicles seemed to have stopped too. He then cited the registration number of one of the police cars that had tailed him: G411 SHA. The Scottish surveillance team had itself been surveyed.

'The trouble with Stephen,' Roderick complained, 'is that he's not prepared to let sleeping dogs lie.'

Nan Clark's diary records:

Sounded genuinely concerned what he ought to

do, which is why he said he was on his way to see me last night. He didn't know what was best to be done. If he went to police Grandma (and family) would have all the pain of the trial. I said what he did was for him to choose. He was living his life and knew what it was like. He couldn't run his life to suit an eighty-year-old woman. It was his life. Where was he going now, was he coming back? No, as planned he would set off to South at weekend. I said take care.

Just as Roderick was preparing to sail from Boulogne, out towards the Atlantic, in the *Austral Soma*, so Detective Superintendent Paul Marks was conferring at Heathrow with Philip Bailhache QC, Jersey's Attorney-General. The island's top lawyer was anxious to hear the tape recording for himself. Having done so, however, he remained cautious. It was impossible for him to make a balanced judgement, he said, on the basis of a recording of such poor quality. So arrangements were made for the tape to be played on more sophisticated equipment which eliminated much of the background noise. Then the Attorney-General was in no doubt. For on Friday 17 July, three days after the clandestine recording, he authorized the issue of a warrant for Roderick's arrest. The document, signed by Lieutenant-Bailiff Jurat the Hon John Coutanche, was quite explicit: Roderick Innes Nelson Newall was wanted for the murder of his parents on or about 10 October 1987. But by the time the necessary legal procedures had been completed, the subject of the warrant had already put to sea, together with his one-man crew, Stephen Beldham.

The Assistant Chief Officer of the Jersey force, Bob Le Breton, had already decided to take a calculated risk of his own, convinced that the time had come for a touch of *glasnost* at Rouge Bouillon. Having called in the editor of the *Jersey Evening Post*, along with other members of the local media, he informed them of the significant developments in the case against Roderick Newall. He hoped that if he took them into his confidence and provided them with inside information they would be more rather than less likely to keep it secret if requested so to do. Far better that, he thought, than to run the risk of there being a leak from within the force, with possibly disastrous results for the entire operation. It was a judgement which was to serve his interests well.

At the States of Jersey police headquarters, the Newall incident room, which had long since ceased to exist, was hastily resurrected, and allocated more spacious premises. For over three years there had been virtually no activity on the case at all. Witness statements and affidavits, together with thousands of other documents, had been filed away in cabinets where they had begun to gather dust. Suddenly everything changed. The incident room was bustling once again, for up to a dozen officers had been drafted in to work full time on the case. To begin with, they all shared a brief which could hardly have been more clear-cut: find Roderick Newall. The hunt was on.

'We used to refer to the tapes as the Crown Jewels,'

Detective Sergeant Charles MacDowall recalls.

> The incident room had the most tremendous buzz
> to it. We all used to come in early and leave at
> eleven o'clock at night. And even then you didn't
> really want to go home. We thought Roderick
> might do a Ronnie Biggs and go to Brazil. Others
> said that he was more likely to be heading back to
> the Falklands, where he was going to set up in
> business. The truth was though that we had no
> idea where he was off to at all.

Like most police officers in Jersey, Charles MacDowall
had been involved in the Newall inquiry several years
earlier. Then working within the fraud squad, his task
had been to investigate Elizabeth and Nicholas
Newall's financial affairs. What he had found was of
considerable interest in that it suggested a possible
motive for the murders, a concept with which the police
had always had great difficulty. It was that in 1985
Nicholas Newall had been advised that his syndicate at
Lloyds, the Outhwaite syndicate number 317/661, had
been exposed to massive environmental and asbestos-
linked claims in the USA. Two years later, and just a
few months before the Newalls' disappearance, the
Financial Times was reporting that these claims were
likely to run to almost £250 million.

Charles MacDowall explains:

> These losses must have worried the Newalls very
> much, because it would have had a considerable

impact on their capital – to the tune of a minimum of £30,000 per annum for at least twenty years – until the claims were met in full. But Nicholas Newall had had the foresight – although perhaps in this context that is not the most appropriate word – to take out an Estate Protection Policy – which meant that should he die all calls on his estate would be met in full. In other words that neither son would be liable to meet these losses should they come to inherit. So you can see that this was a very important aspect of the case.

Not that financial matters were top of the agenda during the summer of 1992. Interpol, the International Criminal Police Commission, based in France, was contacted through London to see if they might be able to assist in tracking down Roderick. After all, it was precisely the sort of case which fell within their remit. But they singularly failed to come up trumps. Then a request was made to the European Customs Union's surveillance aircraft in the hope that their advanced technology and eavesdropping capacity might be used to detect the precise location of the *Austral Soma*. But no help was forthcoming from that quarter. Nor was Seaclaim, a private company specializing in the tracing of stolen yachts, able to offer anything concrete, despite being supplied with a picture, a brochure and every other particular of the *Austral Soma*. For those working in the incident room at Rouge Bouillon, while there was seldom any shortage of excitement, it was nevertheless a very frustrating time. Where on earth was their man?

The police then decided to focus in on the activities of Mark Newall, assuming that the brothers were bound to be in touch before long. Two facts were established without much difficulty: that Mark had an accommodation address in London – BCM 2724 – and that the *Austral Soma* was a British registered vessel whose legal documents had been sent to that address only after Roderick's hasty departure from England. When the company responsible for the accommodation address was contacted by the Jersey police they were prepared to waive their normal rules of confidentiality and revealed that once a month they were forwarding all correspondence to Mark's apartment in Paris. Other sources disclosed that Mark had been staying at Blakes Hotel, in South Kensington, one of London's most exclusive hotels, where each room has its own individual style of décor. Its sophistication must have appealed greatly to Mark, for he had stayed there on fifty-four separate visits in one year alone.

It was a lead which one of the police officers from the Jersey team, Sandra Genee, decided to pursue. She soon succeeded in recruiting to her cause Detective Constable Stephen Kibble of Kensington CID, who made various inquiries at Blakes Hotel on her behalf.

Charles MacDowall explains:

This was a vital contact, because we found out that Mark was due to stay there again. In fact he had faxed ahead to the hotel asking them to send a courier to collect mail from the accommodation address, whereas previously everything was being sent on to Paris. Mark only stayed one night at Blakes, from where we learned that he had phoned a number in America at ten-thirty p.m. their time. Sandra then made contact with the FBI asking them to inform us what that number was. We were told it was Air France's offices in New York. We thought that that was a rather strange call to have made at such an hour. We also established that Mark had booked a number of flights – and flew from Heathrow to Paris, Paris to Madrid, and then Madrid to Tangier. We became convinced that he was carrying the legal documents for the *Austral Soma* and that he was going to hand them to Roderick in Tangier.

It was an astute assessment. For Detective Inspector Martin Fitzgerald, who had been involved in the Newall inquiry from the outset, then received a telephone call from Emma-Jane Lonsdale, whose car and flat Roderick had used during his stay in the UK. She disclosed that Roderick, never shy when it came to contact with the opposite sex, had invited her to join him in Tangier. This confirmed the detective work already carried out by the Jersey force. Nor would it have been his first visit to the Moroccan port, less than twenty miles from the southern tip of Spain.

It was the first major breakthrough since Roderick had eluded the Scottish surveillance team nineteen days earlier. It was agreed that it was important to have a

167

representative of the Jersey force as near to the suspect as possible, and so it was arranged that Detective Sergeant Charles MacDowall would fly to Gibraltar to liaise with the Royal Gibraltar Police, with the aim of locating Roderick in Morocco.

'As far as I was concerned the idea of asking for the assistance of the Royal Navy was pie in the sky,' MacDowall admits.

But Assistant Chief Officer Barry Simpson had already put the wheels in motion, contacting both the office of the Lieutenant-Governor in Jersey and the Ministry of Defence in London. When I arrived in Gibraltar I was met by DI Louis Wink. He said to me that if we didn't get permission from the Royal Navy, then we would have to get ourselves another boat, even if we had to get a rowing boat! I had visions of us rowing across the Atlantic with Roderick under arrest.

Both police officers agreed that it would be a good idea to establish a forward-observation point in Tangier. Two men from Gibraltar's drug squad volunteered to go there under cover and without seeking the authority or approval of the Moroccan government. They were instructed to act as if they were on holiday, but while in the ancient port city they were to both find the *Austral Soma* and identify its young owner.

Having bribed a guard at the main gate to the marina, the officers spotted Roderick's yacht easily enough. They then headed off to find a hotel from where they would be able to keep it under twenty-four-hour observation. Confident that they had found a room affording a suitable view of the vessel, they were nevertheless thwarted when the hotel's receptionist immediately refused to let them have it on the grounds that it had a double bed. Only a room with two singles, he insisted, would be appropriate accommodation for the two men. Having food brought to the room and taking turns to sleep in their single beds, each officer would focus his binoculars on the steel-hulled schooner, scanning its deck for any sign of activity.

Meanwhile, formal approval came through from London: the Royal Navy was indeed prepared to assist. The crew of the patrol boat HMS *Ranger* was standing by and waiting for instructions as to when to proceed. HMS *Argonaut*, a frigate armed with Exocet missiles, and on a courtesy visit to Gibraltar, might also be made available, although minor engine problems were being attended to on this more powerful vessel. The Royal Gibraltar Police firearms team had likewise been briefed and put on stand-by. This elite squad had been trained at Hereford in the best traditions of the SAS.

'Just as we were being told that movement had been detected on board the *Austral Soma*, our communications system went on the blink, and we lost touch with our people in Tangier,' remembers Charles MacDowall. There was also another problem:

I think that the hotel's staff had become suspicious; one of the two Gibraltarian officers was constantly on the phone to us from the public

169

phone in the main reception area, and speaking in Spanish all the time. We thought that they might have been arrested, because there was no contact at all for one hour. We began to discuss plans to hire a plane with a view to flying in other officers to Tangier. But just as we were doing this we suddenly regained communication, and were told that the *Austral Soma* was topping up with fuel and ready to leave.

Time, therefore, for the Royal Navy also to set to sea. Commander Tim Appleyard welcomed Charles Mac-Dowall and the five members of the crack firearms team on board HMS *Ranger*. But on seeing the ship's radar system, on which there appeared to be an enormous amount of activity, the policeman from Jersey was not at all optimistic about the chances of encountering Roderick at sea. Nor had the officers working under cover in Tangier been able to provide any hints as to the direction in which he might be heading. In fact their final message, after they had trailed the *Austral Soma* out along the coastal road from Tangier, could hardly have been more vague. 'Left, left, left,' they relayed back to Gibraltar, 'and out into the Atlantic.'

As the *Ranger* went about its task of checking boats, darkness began to fall. Then, suddenly, at a little after one-thirty a.m., a powerful search beam was shone into the bridge of the Royal Navy vessel, obliging the Gibraltarian firearms officers to crouch down quickly so as not to be seen. For a few seconds everyone was blinded, as the source of the light was only some two hundred yards away. Night-sights revealed that it was Roderick Newall, as always surveillance-conscious, even when sailing the high seas. To put him at ease, the Commander sought to give the impression that they were checking all vessels in the area; that there was nothing out of the ordinary about such activity. Meanwhile, contact was made with police headquarters in Gibraltar, via which a message was relayed back to Rouge Bouillon. There the excitement was running at fever pitch. They were closing in on their man.

'The *Argonaut* had been scrambled by this time,' Charles MacDowall explains.

At first light the following morning we transferred to that frigate. I thought that the boats would simply stop. But they don't – they keep going at quite high speeds, just bringing a transfer vessel alongside and providing you with a rope to climb up. The whole experience was giving me the most enormous buzz. It probably wouldn't have been the most sensible thing to have done, but I really did feel as if I could have walked on water.

The ship's captain, Bob Stevens, announced the strategy he had in mind. He would proceed into international waters, position himself alongside the *Austral Soma* and then inform Roderick that he was under arrest for murder. It was, however, an approach with which Charles MacDowall disagreed. Unlike everyone else on board, he was aware that Roderick had referred to a plan for his suicide come the day of his capture. He

171

had said so explicitly on the tapes. A better plan, the police officer suggested, would be to pretend to be carrying out a routine procedure, such as a check for drugs. Once agreed, the approach was rehearsed in more detail. The most satisfactory place at which to make the arrest would be on the ship's stern side, just behind the helicopter hangars, as it was a flat, open area offering plenty of room to manoeuvre. As these discussions were taking place, the *Argonaut* was continuing to trail Roderick's Canadian-built vessel, five or six miles to his stern.

With the crew of the *Argonaut* operating at 'zulu stations', a heightened state of alert, the Royal Navy began its approach towards the *Austral Soma*. An attempt was made to make contact by radio, but there was initially no reply. However, the sound of the ship's horn must have stirred Roderick, for he then came on the airwaves himself, to be told that the *Argonaut* was empowered by a higher authority to stop and search vessels in the area. That part of their dialogue to date was perfectly true. For international maritime law allows for the Royal Navy to board any ship flying the Red Ensign, which denotes British registration, and such a flag was displayed by the *Austral Soma*.

'What is the name of your captain?' a Royal Navy spokesman asked.

'Roderick Newall.'

Invited to come to the *Argonaut* to have his documentation inspected, Roderick suggested that an emissary be sent to him. It was time for a departure from the truth, exactly as rehearsed. That was impossible, he was informed, because the Royal Navy frigate had been damaged by some flotsam while carrying out checks on another vessel earlier that day. It might have seemed an unlikely story, but it seemed to do the trick.

'It was all very gentlemanly,' says Charles MacDowall, who goes on to explain:

> Then we saw activity on deck. A rowing boat was put in the water and this bloke started rowing. I identified Roderick and saw that he had grown a beard. It seemed to take him about five minutes to come to us, because even though it was a lovely day there was still quite a swell. They then put a ladder down on the port side of the boat for him to climb up.

Once on board Roderick was met by a Royal Navy officer who was wearing a bulletproof vest under his shirt. He proceeded to walk the visitor round towards the deck, and as he did so found that he only had one thing to say. It was an impromptu remark that had not featured in the earlier rehearsal: 'Boy, have we got a surprise for you.'

They had indeed. For as those words were spoken five officers from the Royal Gibraltar Police appeared and surrounded Roderick in a semicircle, with his back facing the sea. They were all dressed in black, special forces style, and one of them was carrying a Heckler & Koch nine-millimetre machine-gun, the other four handguns, but each man's weapon was aimed at Roderick. Royal Navy personnel, also armed, positioned

173

themselves towards the stern of the boat to provide additional cover. With live Exocet missiles on board, their brief had been to take no chances whatsoever.

Ordered to lie flat on the deck, Roderick refused. The command was repeated. And then again. Still he refused, all the time defiantly edging his way towards the armed officers. Moving swiftly to the side of their suspect, one of the firearms team kicked his legs away from him. As Roderick fell flat on his face on the deck he was searched and promptly handcuffed, with his hands behind his back.

Then Detective Sergeant Charles MacDowall stepped forward, armed only with a warrant for Roderick's arrest. Speaking on behalf of the States of Jersey police, he said: 'Roderick Newall, you are under arrest for murder. You are not obliged to say anything unless you wish to do so. But anything you say may be put into writing and given in evidence.'

It was true that it had taken the Jersey police the best part of five years to arrest their man, but he had been arrested nonetheless.

'He was certainly very surprised,' recalls the captain of the *Argonaut*. 'Speechless I would say. It was an unusual operation for us, but one in which we were glad to have been able to assist.'

Led away to a storeroom with an armed naval guard at the door, Roderick found himself in the company of the police officer who had arrested him. He was not lost for words when sitting alone with Charles MacDowall. There were even flashes of the old bravado, for he said how he would have rammed the warship with his yacht had he known that he was being led into a trap. And why, once he had realized he was trapped, had he been so keen to approach the armed officers? Because he was weighing up whether it was worth his while making a grab for a gun. Roderick Newall: a daredevil to the end.

'I had had visions of someone getting shot at one stage,' Charles MacDowall admits.

> But once it was over he didn't cause any trouble. Nor did he become emotional at all. He would just sit and stare into space, as if he had gone off into a world of his own. I spent my time nannying him in a way, providing blankets, cups of tea and so on. We developed a rapport together and he began to say things which weren't in his best interests at all.

It was this very inability to refrain from speaking about his role in the murders that had led to his arrest in the first place. Then, recalling his training in the techniques of interrogation, he would suddenly withdraw again. 'I must remember,' he said, 'not to fall in love with the hand that feeds me.'

The operational plan had only ever extended to returning Roderick to Gibraltar, not Jersey, even though it might well have suited the prosecuting authorities for it to have been otherwise. Once there on that tiny British patch of Spain's Mediterranean coast, he was immediately rearrested under a separate warrant issued by the

Royal Gibraltar police. The dazed prisoner needed no prompting to realize that it was high time to make contact with his lawyer, David Le Quesne, in Jersey. He eventually managed to get through to him on his ex-directory number at his home in the parish of St Clement. At the end of that conversation he turned to those around him and announced that it was his intention to return to the island as soon as possible.

'When I went to bed that night I hadn't slept for two days,' Charles MacDowall concludes.

But I still couldn't get to sleep. It was the most tremendous experience; an emotional one too. Because both boys had always been very arrogant. They seemed to think that all policemen were thick, and of Jersey policemen in particular as somehow having straw between their teeth. Roderick could not bring himself to believe that the Jersey police had gone to the trouble of mobilizing the Royal Navy and come to arrest him in the middle of the Atlantic Ocean. Nor, in a sense, could I. You might have expected such an operation from the Met in London. But not from our small team in St Helier. Yet together we had pulled it off.

At Rouge Bouillon the atmosphere was one of elation. Of course mistakes had been made during the course of the previous five years. Of course, with the benefit of hindsight, they would have done things differently. But all that now belonged firmly to the past. For the States of Jersey police, here, finally, was a dramatic arrest unprecedented in the island's history. Roderick Newall had evaded the Scottish surveillance team. But twenty-two days later he had been duped into rowing his way back into the arms of the Jersey police. Having allowed his guard to slip for a moment, he had made an error of judgement which was to cost him dear.

9

'Better Alive in Jersey Than Dead in Gibraltar'

'Gibraltar – or "Gib" as it's affectionately known – is a rare gem. Jutting into the cerulean Strait which separates two vastly different continents by a whisper of 8 miles, it is the place where the warm waters of the Mediterranean converge with the Atlantic. This inimitable position has enticed invaders to these shores for centuries, leaving behind a vibrant history and a character that displays the diverse cultures that have dominated Gibraltar throughout the ages.'

All no doubt perfectly true. But the view of Gibraltar promoted by its Department of Tourism was certainly not a perspective shared by Roderick Newall. For he now found himself in circumstances which could scarcely have been more inhospitable or austere, locked up in the medieval Moorish Castle Prison. Built during the conquest of the Iberian Peninsula, and

179

displaying the scars of the fourteen sieges it has with-
stood, it seldom gets a mention in any of the 'Rock's'
promotional literature.

Aware that Roderick would need a talented local
lawyer with whom he would be able to liaise in any
future extradition proceedings, David Le Quesne contacted Chris Finch to ask him to represent his client's
interests. A former RAF officer and member of the
Royal Gibraltar Police before going on to study for the
Bar, Finch had already enjoyed a high profile, having
acted for the families of three IRA members shot dead
in the colony by British security forces. Delighted to
accept the Newall brief, he wasted no time in springing
into action.

'There was unnecessary brutality,' he complained in
Gibraltar's Magistrates Court, 'in the arrest of Roderick Newall. This was the closest one can get to modern
piracy. Was it really necessary to bring him back here
trussed up like a chicken?'

Nor was Finch happy with the conditions of Roderick's confinement, for it had soon became clear that he
was being treated as a high-security prisoner, being
kept in virtual solitary confinement and having all his
telephone calls monitored.

Roderick did not need much prompting. The tactic
might not have achieved a great deal during his sojourn
in Jersey's prison at La Moye, but the former soldier
announced that he would register his protest by beginning an indefinite hunger strike, refusing all solid food.
Uncomfortable in the glare of publicity, it took Stipendiary Magistrate Felix Pizzarello just five days to order

an immediate investigation of the allegedly poor conditions. It was a minor success for Roderick within the framework of a penal regime which he regarded as deliberately discriminating against him.

However sweet the taste of victory might have been, it could not have lingered for very long. For on Wednesday 9 September 1992, five weeks to the day since his arrest on the high seas, Roderick slashed his wrists and groin with a razor blade which had been smuggled into his cell. By the time the authorities reached their prisoner they found him hiding under his sheets, where he had lain bleeding for over an hour and a half, losing six pints of blood. A few minutes more and he would undoubtedly have died. As he was rushed to the intensive care unit of St Bernard's Hospital, a thorough search of his cell was carried out. It took little time to discover a small amount of cocaine. He had informed his uncle and aunt when visiting them at the Dunkeld House Resort Hotel in the middle of July that he would not hesitate to take his own life rather than spend his best years in prison. He had come perilously close to keeping his pledge.

Nan Clark was at her home in Alicante, southern Spain, when she heard of her nephew's attempted suicide. She immediately flew from Valencia to Málaga, from where she hired a car and headed off along the coastal road towards Gibraltar. She recalls:

When I saw Roderick he looked to me as though he was on drugs, and I don't mean medical drugs. Of course by this stage I knew that he had killed my sister. The only way that I could deal with this was to try to divide my mind and say that I am visiting my nephew; that he remains Elizabeth's child no matter what, and that she would still have expected me to look after him to the best of my ability.

Having checked in at Gibraltar's Holiday Inn, Nan Clark was accompanied to the hospital by Detective Sergeant Charles MacDowall, the arresting officer on board HMS *Argonaut*. When they got there, officials, guards, nurses and lawyers seemed to appear from each and every direction; hardly the ideal setting for a hospital visit, let alone a heart-to-heart talk. Nan Clark's diary records:

Roderick pale, shocked. Two police in ward, one in corridor. R seemed almost alarmed and then pleased. Finch arrived out of blue and stood at foot of bed. Received instructions, then left. Would I go and see Finch to see what I thought of him? Started to talk about his prison conditions but was immediately stopped by one of the guards. Nurse asked me to leave. Visited R again about 5.30. Meantime had visited Finch. Not impressed. Said so to R. Gave him some books. Worried about his dressings. Left shortly afterwards. Decided to drop R a line to explain what I felt and also to tell him that he could go to Jersey immediately if he so wished, contrary to what Finch was saying. Asked him to consider. Back to hospital

again. Not quite up to UK standards! Ants on
floor etc. Saw deep cut left arm. Worried about
septicaemia in leg wound caused as they tried to
transfuse. Later seemed better in himself, so I left
for London more cheerful. Spoke to Mark who is
in States. Read him my notes on trip. As usual M
disagreed with everything. Asked him to phone
Detective Inspector Adamson. He said look where
talking had got Roderick. Said he did not trust me
etc.

Within two days of his aunt's departure for London
Roderick was back in his cell and writing to her. He
was anxious to respond to the various points she had
raised. He first of all apologized for not having been
more forthcoming, explaining that he shared her feeling of inhibition among crowds of people. Despite the
reservations of his lawyer, he had agreed to see a
psychiatrist. But he could not bring himself to accept
his aunt's advice, and had made up his mind to remain
in Gibraltar and fight his case. For in his view its legal
system was more like Britain's, and he certainly saw no
prospect of a fair trial in Jersey. The letter ended on a
note of concern for Mark. When he last spoke with
him, he explained, his younger brother was in the USA
and, presumably as a result of what he was going
through, was unable to work properly.

In the basement of Jersey's La Hougue Bie Museum at
Grouville, there was a mixture of excitement and
apprehension. An employee had discovered what

appeared to be the remains of a human leg. And since nobody seemed able to account for how the leg might have got there, or suggest where the other parts of the body to which it had once been attached might be, it was agreed that the best course of action would be to ring the police. At Rouge Bouillon the call was immediately put through to the Newall incident room.

At the request of the police, the pathology department at St Helier's General Hospital carried out a careful examination of the find. It was unmistakably a human leg, but doctors working there were reluctant to commit themselves on whether or not the bones might have been those of either Elizabeth or Nicholas Newall. The best thing to do, they suggested, was to have the various parts carbon-dated. And the best place to carry out such a test was Oxford University. Without further delay, the bones were placed in a sealed box which was then wrapped in polystyrene and paper. As Detective Inspector Martin Fitzgerald and Detective Constable Charles Canham happened to be leaving Jersey for RAF Brize Norton, in Oxfordshire, on other business related to the Newall inquiry, it was hoped that they might be prepared to include the package among their other luggage and make a brief detour to the university.

The two detectives had a far longer journey ahead of them. They were bound for the Falkland Islands, where they were anxious to speak to Jérôme Poncet, the explorer to whom Roderick had become particularly close. Aware that they knew very little about Roderick's years in the Falklands, the Jersey police wondered if there might not be somebody down there in the South Atlantic with whom he had shared his secret. This was considerably more than idle speculation, for Roderick had stated quite clearly during the tape-recorded conversation with Stephen and Gay Newall that there was one other person outside of the immediate family who knew of his guilt, although he had not named that individual. Perhaps it was Poncet. Whatever the case, with Roderick's defence team threatening to contest the admissibility of the tape, the lead had to be checked.

While Roderick was continuing to recover from his suicide attempt, the two Jersey policemen were flying courtesy of the RAF via Ascension Island towards Port Stanley, in the Falkland Islands, where they were escorted in by Tornado fighter jets. Setting about their inquiries, they soon found that their suspect had been very popular with the local population. They also found that since their visit had been announced in advance by the press, many people were reluctant to be seen to be co-operating too closely with the police. In that respect Jersey and the Falkland Islands are alike: there tends to be a closing of ranks among both groups of islanders when outsiders are perceived as intruding, with word of the potential threat spreading very fast. Detective Constable Canham recalls:

When Jérôme Poncet heard that we were on our way he immediately contacted his lawyer. Other people did so too. First of all he agreed to see us but then changed his mind. We thought that we would go and see him on Beaver Island, which he owns, but he informed us that he would refuse the helicopter permission to land. While we did find out a lot more about Roderick's life out there and filled in an important gap, we really left empty-handed. I must say that it was a hell of a long way to go to try to interview somebody. Nor did our mystery leg prove to have anything to do with the case. Tests revealed that the bones were not five but thousands of years old and dated back to Egyptian times.

In Gibraltar's Magistrates Court legal battle was about to commence. To those looking in from the outside, however, the sudden heightening of security suggested preparations for a battle of an altogether different kind. Acting on information that an attempt might be made to assist Roderick to escape from custody, the entire Royal Gibraltar firearms team was deployed to escort him from Moorish Castle Prison to the court-room in Main Street. Its members dressed in paramili-tary gear and armed with sub-machine-guns capable of firing six hundred rounds a minute, the motorcade sped the prisoner to the court, outside which bundles of barbed wire had been hastily deployed. It was a most unconventional setting for extradition proceedings.

Inside the courtroom the atmosphere was equally tense. Speaking for the Crown, Desmond de Silva QC argued that there was overwhelming evidence against Roderick, certainly sufficient to extradite him from Gibraltar to Jersey. De Silva knew very well that his trump card was the tape recorded at the Dunkeld House Resort Hotel, whereas much of the other evidence against Roderick was merely circumstantial.

'It is the case of the Crown,' the eloquent silk argued, 'that Roderick Newall was an assassin of his parents.' He went on:

> It is further the case of the Crown that just under five years later, as this accused gazed into the face of his father's identical twin, there spilled from his lips the pent-up guilt that he had harboured for so long, and which finally broke its banks in a series of admissions that point inescapably to the conclusion that he is responsible for patricide and matricide. These matters amount to the clearest confession to being involved in murder that a person could make without saying, "Yes, I did it."

The argument put by the defence was that whatever their content the tapes ought to be deemed inadmissible. Already under suspicion for murder, Roderick Newall ought to have been cautioned before participating in any interview conducted in order to gather evidence against him, just as he would have been had the police been conducting the interview themselves. Stephen and Gay Newall, Chris Finch argued, were for all practical purposes an extension of the police while talking with their nephew at the Perthshire hotel. And in any event, the words of the tape did not point to his client being a murderer: they were merely consistent with the defendant's desire to cover up for another. It was not a confession at all.

Finch further submitted that the uncle and aunt's words, honeyed though they were, were despicable in that they were deliberately calculated to lead to an unwary admission. It was all part of a huge fraud, a violation of his client's rights, a conspiracy by the police and Stephen Newall to get what they could not have otherwise obtained if the defendant's right to silence had been honoured. It was a powerful argument and well put. The Stipendiary Magistrate then retired to consider his decision.

Important though the legal issues undoubtedly were, they were of little interest to the general public, who were more interested in the high drama of the courtroom appearances. And there were a number of women, it seemed, who were interested only in Roderick. Detective Inspector Jimmy Adamson, involved in the case from the outset, could not make head nor tail of their devotion to the accused:

He's been receiving dozens of letters from female admirers in Britain. And in increasing bundles too. I don't know what it is, but every time his photograph appears in newspapers, handcuffed and being escorted to court, it seems to strike a feminine chord. Many ladies point out that he is very good looking and appears to have a boyish charm.

Roderick also appeared to be enjoying a good deal of luck. For, despite the very strong case against him, the magistrate ruled that the tapes were indeed inadmissible, because, as he put it, 'they had been obtained in a sneaky way', thereby 'circumventing', as he put it, Roderick's legal right to silence. It was a stunning victory for the defence team. And for a few hours it looked as if the handsome high-security prisoner was likely to walk away from the court a free man, no doubt to be hailed as a hero by the ever-growing ranks of his female fan club. Visions of setting sail again in the *Austral Soma* were rekindled; plans for his chartering business to the Antarctic revived. Then Gibraltar's Supreme Court intervened and put a damper on both of these projects, by agreeing to a judicial review of the magistrate's decision.

Paul Marks was sitting in the public gallery of the Magistrates Court when Felix Pizzarello read out his judgement on the tapes. 'I felt physically sick,' Marks recalls. 'The UK press were packed into court and started shouting out to Roderick as soon as the magistrate retired. I knew immediately that a card which I had hoped not to have to play was now needed before the judicial review took place.'

It was just as well, therefore, that Detective Inspector Jimmy Adamson had not been sitting on his hands. The last thing that he or any other Jersey police officer had wanted was a lengthy legal battle. The case had already taken up far too much of their time. It had been clear as soon as complex legal arguments about the tapes had begun that they were in for a fierce contest over extradition, and they realized that the additional time which this allowed them could be put to good use. At least now they knew precisely where their man was, that he was unlikely to be going very far, and that therefore a unique opportunity existed not just to carefully review all the evidence already accumulated against Roderick Newall but also to produce further depositions. This was precisely why, during the weeks before the unexpected judgement in Gibraltar, Jimmy Adamson had been listening to the tape-recorded confession time and again. And the more he did so the more convinced he became that the other person to whom Roderick had unburdened himself was a woman.

After Roderick's arrest at sea, a thorough search had been carried out of the *Austral Soma*. Among the items found on the yacht was a Filofax in which all of Roderick's contacts were listed. (One of the first battles in Gibraltar Magistrates Court concerned a request from Chris Finch for the Magistrate to order its return to Roderick.) Jimmy Adamson examined the names and telephone numbers carefully. Because he had spent several years on the case, many of them were already familiar to him; school friends, army friends, girlfriends. His eyes eventually settled on one particular entry, Helena Pedo, a name he had not heard mentioned before. Next to it was a number which he soon discovered was in Brazil. No reply. No reply. No reply again. And then, finally, armed with a new area dialling code, success.

Roderick had met Helena Pedo during the summer of 1991 when, having sailed the Atlantic single-handed, he arrived in Pôrto Alegre, a city situated at the junction of five rivers and the capital of the state of Rio Grande do Sul, in southern Brazil. An attractive divorcee in her thirties with three children of her own, she worked as an English teacher and interpreter. Their romance had proceeded at a rapid pace, for within a few weeks Roderick had been invited to move into her flat. Here was the woman Roderick had written to Nan Clark about with such evident warmth and enthusiasm.

But was she aware, Jimmy Adamson asked Helena Pedo, that Roderick had recently been arrested for the murder of his parents? No, she was not. Her tone, however, appeared to indicate that this news came as no great surprise. The reason for this soon became clear. Roderick had initially told her that his parents had merely disappeared, but as their relationship had strengthened he had admitted to her that he was responsible for their deaths. And she then proceeded to describe in detail the precise contents of what had been said. Adamson, with his tape recorder running at the incident room at Rouge Bouillon, could hardly believe his ears.

Delighted with this breakthrough, and convinced that he had been handed a bright new key to the mystery, he repeated a journey that was familiar to him, rushing to knock on Detective Superintendent Paul Marks's door. The head of Jersey's CID listened to the tape and saw right away its enormous evidential value. So did the island's Attorney-General, although he cast doubt on Helena Pedo's being

prepared to appear as a witness for the prosecution.
Paul Marks explains:

> I encouraged Jimmy to develop a rapport with
> Helena Pedo, and they had a number of phone
> calls together. This became quite an expensive
> business because, boy, could she talk. She was
> worried, though. If she was threatened, would we
> be able to protect her? Yes, but only if she did as
> we told her. While we didn't want to expose her to
> any danger, we knew that we had to see her pretty
> quickly, because we knew that Roderick must
> have been aware of the danger she presented to
> him. She needed a lot of persuading. We said that
> we would fly her to London. But she insisted that
> we had to see her in Brazil if we were to see her at
> all. Also, we were worried about Roderick's fight
> to get his Filofax back. Who did he need to contact
> so urgently?

Unlike the earlier police trip to the Falklands, which
had been announced in advance by the press, this time
elaborate steps were taken to ensure secrecy. Helena
Pedo had insisted on it herself. Flights were paid for on
personal credit cards, inoculations were settled in cash
rather than invoiced to the police and for those who
might happen to ask, the official line was that both
Marks and Adamson were on inquiries in the UK. At
Rouge Bouillon the era of *glasnost* had passed.

On Tuesday 13 October 1992, in the early hours of
the morning, the two police officers arrived in São

Paulo. Helena Pedo had agreed to fly up from Pôrto Alegre later that evening in order to join them at the Cad'oro, a hotel built in the Portuguese colonial style and situated on the edge of the city's red-light district. Exhausted from their journey, the detectives were desperate to catch up on some sleep.

'I was a bit paranoid about catching malaria,' Paul Marks admits.

So I had bought a large mosquito net for the bed, sprays, electrical devices, adaptors and so on. I erected the tent, got the fumes going nicely in the room, and sprayed myself all over. I felt quite comfortable, although the tent soon began to collapse on me. Jimmy Adamson was peeved because he hadn't brought a net and his electric fume device was the wrong voltage. I said: 'Forget it, you're not sleeping in my bed.' After a few hours' sleep a maid knocked on the door, let herself in and started shouting and laughing in fits. São Paulo had apparently been clear of malaria for twenty years.

That evening Marks and Adamson settled down in the hotel's lobby to await the arrival of their prospective key witness.

'Every time a girl came in we looked over her shoulder to see how she was signing in,' recalls Marks. 'We must have looked like a right couple of perverts. We waited and waited, but she didn't turn up. I thought that the whole thing was a waste of time and said as much to Jimmy. Six thousand miles for nothing. I was furious.'

The following morning Adamson spoke to Helena Pedo on the telephone from the Consulate. Her explanation was disarmingly simple. She had changed her mind about the interview. 'Look,' the Detective Inspector interrupted her, 'we are coming to see you. We are knocking on your door.'

And with those words he terminated their conversation. He then realized that he had not sought the authority of his boss, who happened to be standing next to him, nor indeed did he have any idea of precisely where in Brazil her door might be. Marks checked with the Vice Consul that their authority extended to Pôrto Alegre, and agreed to Adamson's impromptu arrangements. The British High Commission promptly arranged for the honorary Vice Consul for Pôrto Alegre to meet the police officers on their arrival at the city's airport. The High Commissioner's driver whisked the two Jersey police officers to São Paulo's airport for the two-hour flight.

Paul Marks remembers:

I spotted this chap right away. Six foot two, typical ex pat Brit from a Graham Greene novel, cattle baron and so on. He gave us a quick tutorial on the nature of the Brazilian woman. He said that they needed to be treated politely and that they played hard to get. We needed to make her feel important. It was something akin to a process of seduction. We told him all about the case, thinking that he was a pretty safe bet, being some six thousand miles away. Then he casually mentioned that he happened to know the chair of the National Cattle Bureau for Jersey Cows, a friend of his and an acquaintance of mine. I realized right away the risk to security and braced myself for the leak back home.

Having reserved a room in a hotel in Pôrto Alegre, Jimmy Adamson phoned Helena Pedo again. He repeated his earlier approach, announcing that he would shortly be arriving at her flat.

'No, don't do that,' she replied. 'I'll come to your hotel.'

She was dropped off by her father, a local lawyer. The two policemen made a direct appeal: 'Look, we've come all this way, at least let us take you out for dinner.'

Although she did not have a very high regard for policemen in general, Helena could see that Marks and Adamson were sincere, and accepted their invitation.

As they spruced themselves up for dinner, the two detectives agreed on their strategy for 'seduction'. Adamson would do the talking and drink only water, while Marks would drink wine and encourage Helena to do likewise. There was not much success there, however, for in the event their guest refused any alcohol at all. A smooth performer, Adamson set out his case with confidence and conviction, explaining that even if she was not prepared to testify in court, a statement would be enormously helpful. Any material she might be able to provide would be used only as a last resort and if absolutely necessary. Finally accepting a glass of wine before Paul Marks polished off the whole bottle himself, she began to relax, asking a number of pertinent questions relating to the case. Rapport was established, confidence built up, another bottle of wine ordered and opened. After a slow start, the evening was going well. By the time dessert had been served, all three were talking animatedly about the case, and it was apparent that Helena had reached a verdict. Yes, she confirmed, she would be prepared to make a statement.

Paul Marks admits:

> I only realized afterwards that she had spent the
> whole evening teasing us, playing hard to get, just
> as the Vice Consul had said. She had every inten-
> tion of co-operating with us all along. She had
> even consulted her own lawyer, who had told her
> to follow her conscience. And her conscience had
> been telling her to talk.

The following morning Helena returned to the detec-tives' hotel to make her formal statement. And what a story she had to tell. It had begun over a year earlier, one cold day in July 1991, when sitting together by the fire, Roderick had asked her to get from her bedroom a book which he knew she had. It was *The Glass Bead Game* and written by Hermann Hesse, the German novelist and winner of the Nobel prize for literature. A main theme of the book is man's breaking out of the established modes of existence in search of his essential spirit. When she handed the book to Roderick he immediately turned to page 395. Knowing precisely which paragraph he wanted her to hear, he began to read aloud:

'Oh! he thought in grief and horror, now I am guilty of his death. And only now, when there was no longer need to save his pride or offer resistance, he felt, in shock and sorrow, how dear this man had already become to him. And since in spite of all rational objections he felt responsible for the Master's death, there came over him, with a premonitory shudder of awe, a sense that this guilt would utterly change him and his life, and would demand much greater things of him than he had ever before demanded of himself.'

Roderick had then put the book down, and, with tears streaming down his face, took his girlfriend by the shoulders and kept repeating the same short, simple sentence: 'I am a murderer, I am a murderer, I am a murderer.'

'It was a written statement,' Paul Marks explains, 'which Jimmy was taking down and she was signing page by page. I kept thinking to myself: carry on signing now, don't change your mind.'

She did not. And there was more to follow, as she described how Roderick had gone on to say not just that he was responsible for the murder of his parents, but how very much he regretted it. Only after their deaths had he come to realize how very much his parents were in love with each other. He spoke of the pain and burden of his guilt. And that he had felt

197

compelled to open his heart to her because of how close they had become. He had also spoken of the extent to which he feared going to see Uncle Stephen in Scotland, convinced that he would be unable to maintain his silence in the presence of his father's identical twin.

'I've no doubt that she was in love with Roderick,' Paul Marks says.

> And that Roderick was saying that he wanted to marry her. But that before she made up her mind there were certain things she ought to know. Although she was horrified, at the same time she had wanted to find out more. So she had accompanied him on a trip to Miami in the March of 1992.

There they had gone to see the violent but popular film *Cape Fear*, in which a freed psychopath, played by Robert De Niro, stalks the lawyer who successfully prosecuted the case against him. Helena, whose interests were in language and literature, thought that the film was ghastly. Not so Roderick. He confided to her afterwards that it was good to live in fear. It was at this point that Helena had realized that their relationship was both dangerous and doomed. She suggested to Roderick that he should see a psychiatrist. He replied that he was unable to do that, but that he wanted her to help him to come to terms both with the murders and his own guilt. It was a role which she was not at all eager to assume.

Jimmy Adamson put down his pen. Helena appended her final signature. And Paul Marks breathed an enormous sigh of relief. It was powerful, first-class evidential material. Paul Marks says:

> Once that statement was in the briefcase we were all much more relaxed. We went out for dinner again. She picked us up and showed us around her city, of which she was extremely proud. She also took us to one of the local slums, which I found rather frightening. I said to Jimmy: 'Whatever else you do, just don't part with that briefcase.'

The trip had been a success. The detectives' double act had worked. It was time to return to Jersey.

'We had hoped never to have to call Helena Pedo, but the loss, however temporary, of the tapes from Scotland was a crisis,' says Marks. 'I spoke at length with Philip Bailhache, our Attorney-General – we sat in a children's playground on an RAF base near Gibraltar airport – and he agreed to fund her costs to come to Jersey to swear her deposition before a judge.'

A few days later, when the police produced Helena Pedo's statement as a deposition in the extradition proceedings, the defence team was taken entirely by surprise. Or, as Marks would later put it, they were 'gobsmacked'.

Nor was his ex-girlfriend's statement the only bad news about to come Roderick's way. For that very same week, during the latter part of December 1992, Gibraltar's Chief Justice, Alister Kneller, ruled that the Stipendiary Magistrate, Felix Pizzarello, had erred in law in ruling that the tapes were inadmissible. Once he had concluded that the confession had been given voluntarily, Pizzarello then had no discretion to reject the tapes as evidence in the case. In so doing he had exceeded his powers, encroaching on the jurisdiction of Jersey's Royal Court. So the tapes were admissible after all. Not that that meant that the legal proceedings were over; far from it. With his eyes set on the Judicial Committee of the Privy Council, Chris Finch immediately announced that he was considering an appeal against the appeal.

He might not himself have received any formal instruction in the law, but Roderick could see that the case against him was becoming water-tight. His solution was a familiar enough one: overdosing with sleeping pills smuggled into his cell. Found in a coma, he was rushed once again to St Bernard's Hospital, where he lay unconscious for some time. But within forty-eight hours, late on Christmas day, he began to regain consciousness. If it was indeed another attempt to take his own life, it had ended in failure again.

It seemed that in Moorish Castle Prison almost anything could be smuggled past the guards, despite a series of reviews and a constant tightening up of procedures relating to security. Drugs and razor blades continued to find their way into Roderick's cell. The fact that he was in solitary confinement seemed to make not the slightest difference at all. Ten weeks later a syringe concealed in an orange arrived, the apparatus for suicide attempt number three. For relatives like Nan Clark, who loved Roderick in spite of his sins, watching him deteriorate was an extremely frustrating and painful process, as her diary records:

> Who is supplying Roderick with all of these drugs?
> Some of them aren't even available in Europe. R is
> gradually being destroyed and if kept in Gibraltar
> will be only a shell. Normal life is fading for him.
> Soon nothing of the old R will be left, the best
> gone. Finch encourages R to be antagonistic
> towards authority so destroys the one way he
> usually survives – by making friends with every-
> one. R is looking like a drug addict now. Have
> tried to kick start but I doubt it will be successful.
> No matter consequences, he must be better off
> anywhere else. Have told R I think he is better to
> be alive in Jersey than dead in Gibraltar.

A little before nine a.m. on Wednesday 17 March 1993,
Mark Newall was in his flat in Paris. He expected to be
behind his desk at the Banque Arabe et Internationale
d'Investissement within an hour. He thrived on his
work as a fund manager and was highly respected by all
those around him, just as he had been while working at
Sheppards in St Helier. But he was not to make it to the
office that day.

Paul Marks had been told that he could apply for a
warrant for the arrest of Mark Newall. He was not
concerned about the Attorney-General's reason for
issuing that authority – rather that it should be done
quickly before anyone found out and complications set
in. More secrecy, more documents, more diplomacy,
and more flights lay ahead for the policeman. It was

agreed that Marks, Adamson and MacDowall would oversee the arrest.

That morning French detectives collected the three Jersey officers, and after darting through the early-morning traffic they settled in a parking place on high ground above the entrance to Mark's elegant apartment.

The French officers entered the flat with the assistance of the concierge. A few moments later the Jersey policemen followed suit. There Mark sat, pale and quiet for the moment, handcuffed to one of the fine dining chairs. The lounge of his two-floor apartment was tastefully decorated, two trees were situated within the room, one wall was entirely mirrored and a spiral staircase led from the side of the room to a small roof garden and two bedrooms, each with a bathroom above. The room was dimly lit by the tall, typically Parisian windows.

It did not take Mark long to regain his legendary self-possession.

'I had never met him before,' Paul Marks would later explain.

He didn't know me and I didn't see any reason to introduce myself. But when eventually we did find ourselves together back at the offices of the Brigade Criminelle, I sat at one end of the room and he, handcuffed to another chair at the other, asked me who I was. I told him Detective Superintendent Marks, in charge of the inquiry. To which he retorted: 'I thought you were a chap from the

Embassy looking after my interests.' I remember thinking what an inflated opinion he had of himself.

Mark then tried to establish the credentials of his opponent. He quizzed the Detective Superintendent and in doing so said: 'I suppose you are from England – I haven't heard your name before'. The implication that it would take more than a Jersey policeman to cause such a stir was not at all difficult to detect.

'It gave me some pleasure to assure him I was a Jersey man,' says Marks, and he seemed put out that he had been brought to book by a "Jersey plod", and particularly an overweight one at that.'

He might not have put up a struggle. But inwardly Mark was seething. He had never sought to conceal himself from the police. On the contrary, he had often gone out of his way to inform them of where and when he could be contacted. Was it really necessary to take such dramatic steps against him? What new information could the police possibly have in their possession which appeared to incriminate him? The answer lay in the tapes. Everyone who had listened to them, from the Attorney-General of Jersey to the Chief Justice of Gibraltar, agreed: whatever else Roderick might have said in respect of his own guilt, he was most certainly doing his utmost to cover up for another person. And that other person, the police had concluded, was his younger brother, Mark.

A thorough search was carried out of Mark's apartment, and several items were taken back to

Jersey for tests. There was one piece of paper sitting on the mantelpiece which immediately caught the eye of the island's detectives and required no forensic work at all: the bill for the meal at the Sea Crest Hotel, Elizabeth and Nicholas's last supper, and eaten some five and a half years earlier. What on earth was it doing there?

A few moments later two huge gendarmes, made to look even taller by the pillbox hats they were wearing, handcuffed Mark and walked him away. Marks followed the trio down to the ground floor. Later, on entering the splendid cobbled courtyard of Paris's Palais de Justice, the Detective Superintendent caught sight of Mark sandwiched between the two giant policemen, *en route* to the city's infamous La Santé prison, a far cry from his normal Club Class life. The scene was thus set for a joint appearance with brother Roderick before Jersey's own courts of law.

Unlike the judicial proceedings in Gibraltar, the process of extradition from France was speedy enough. For six weeks later Mark Newall was heading back towards Jersey, the island where he had spent his formative years before being sent off first to prep school and then to Radley. But the police soon found that Mark did not have a lot to say on his return to the island, as Nan Clark's diary reveals:

30th April 1993: Adamson phoned at 4.30 to say that Mark had arrived back in Jersey 20 minutes previously. Had spoken to Le Quesne who said Mark would not talk. Said Le Q was going to see

Rod and try and persuade him against further appeals.

Four days later Mark broke his self-imposed silence. 'Not guilty,' he replied, in Jersey's Police Court, when formally charged with the murder of his parents by St Brelade Centenier Barry Walsh. Now he would fight to clear his name; fight for everything he had achieved. True, he might not have been as tough or as physically fit as his brother, but Mark Newall was to emerge as a formidable adversary indeed.

Fourteen months after he had first agreed to represent Roderick's interests in Gibraltar, Chris Finch was back before the Magistrate, Felix Pizzarello, to whom he said: 'The defence has no submission to make in the committal of my client either on the facts or the law. His defence is to be reserved to such time as when he appears in a court in Jersey.'

The *Jersey Evening Post* put it in plain English in its front-page headlines: 'Extradition: Newall gives up the fight.' It was true. After all the legal wrangling, one hunger strike, four suicide attempts, many months in solitary confinement, a fortune spent on lawyers' fees and levels of security unprecedented in judicial proceedings, Roderick had finally agreed to an uncontested extradition after all. It was precisely what Nan Clark had advised him to do a few weeks after his arrival on the tiny British colony. On 5 November 1993 it was made official. A warrant was issued by Field Marshal Sir John Chapple, Commander in Chief of the City of Gibraltar, and addressed to the governor of

Moorish Castle Prison, ordering that Roderick Innes Nelson Newall be returned to the island of Jersey forthwith. Having himself been attacked by Roderick, the prison governor was delighted to comply with the order. He could not recall the last time he had been so relieved to see a prisoner go.

At Rouge Bouillon the scent of victory was beginning to fill the air. Recently promoted to Assistant Chief Officer, Paul Marks had felt at times that the case was close to overtaking his life, just as it had done to Graham Nimmo's a few years earlier. Marks's remit had been to oversee the running of the whole of Jersey's CID, not to devote all of his time and energy to the Newall inquiry. But the case had become all-consuming. He had made well over a hundred flights in connection with it, hopping from one continent to another. The costs were almost incalculable. Extra budgets had been allocated. Every available penny and more had been spent.

There was certainly the time, energy and funding, however, for one final flight: to escort Roderick Newall back to Jersey. A Citation jet operated by Aviation Beauport Ltd was chartered specifically for this purpose. Detective Inspector Martin Fitzgerald would also be flying out to Gibraltar, together with the brothers' lawyer, David Le Quesne. Soon Roderick and Mark would be reunited within the walls of HM Prison, La Moye – a stone's throw from the scene of the murders.

Paul Marks flew to Gibraltar a couple of days before the deadline. Some strange events there had prompted a degree of caution. In particular, a bugging device had been found in Desmond de Silva's hotel suite.

What was to stop Roderick making suicide attempt number five on board the aeroplane? This issue had begun to weigh on Martin Fitzgerald's mind. Before the flight, therefore, he met the pilot, Captain Greg Graham, to discuss what additional security measures they might be able to introduce. Neither man relished the prospect of Roderick making a dash for the emergency exit. They considered the possibility of handcuffing the prisoner to his seat to prevent him doing so. But that measure would only have raised other issues relating to safety. Eventually it was agreed that Roderick would be seated towards the rear of the aircraft, as far away from the exit as possible, with the Detective Inspector seated next to the exit. Twenty-five years in the Jersey force had exposed Martin Fitzgerald to a wide variety of experiences. But never before had he prepared himself to prevent a man suspected of double murder from hurling himself out of a plane in mid-air.

Roderick's arrival in Gibraltar had been the result of dramatic occurrences. HMS *Argonaut* had seen to that. His departure was to be a little out of the ordinary too, as Captain Graham was about to discover. For the authorities had obtained secret information that there existed a specific threat to their mission. Before the plane's return flight to Jersey, therefore, the Royal Gibraltar police, the army and military intelligence met to see what they could do to counter any such threat. Maybe the reports were true; maybe not. Whatever the case, everybody agreed that one thing was certain: for this operation nothing could be left to chance.

Accordingly, nothing was. The Citation was put in a hangar overnight, with electronic surveillance cones distributed all around and security guards with dogs patrolling the area outside. At five-thirty a.m. on Saturday 6 November, Captain Graham and his co-pilot arrived to prepare the plane for take-off. Neither man had slept very well, aware that armed guards had been posted outside their hotel overnight. The pilots had even been advised to eat only in the hotel's restaurant, to reduce the risk of their food being poisoned. It was hardly surprising that both men reported not only a sudden loss of appetite but also a longing for a return to their more routine charter work, shuttling business executives backwards and forwards between Jersey and France.

Half an hour later the hangar doors were partially opened and a large convoy of vehicles ushered in. Roderick was seated in the last car, handcuffed to Martin Fitzgerald. Then, at seven o'clock, the doors were suddenly opened wide, as air traffic control cleared the jet for take-off while it was still in the hangar. Advised that a sniper attack could not be ruled out, Captain Graham taxied the plane in zigzag fashion out towards the runway and braced himself for a rapid take-off. As they headed up and away from Moorish Castle Prison, the pilot banked sharply over the Rock.

In Jersey the atmosphere was one of intense excitement and anticipation. Press releases were being updated and rewritten every hour. At the island's airport special arrangements had been made in conjunction with the duty terminal manager: a separate

208

area was to be set aside to which the aircraft would make its way for disembarkation. For the press it was a moment not to be missed. Given permission to photograph and film the arriving party during their transfer from the aircraft to the police vehicles already standing by, journalists and camera crews placed themselves where they thought they would be likely to catch Roderick most clearly. The passengers would then head off via the airport's engineering compound towards the police headquarters at Rouge Bouillon. Everything had been thoroughly prepared in advance.

There was not a single shot of sniper fire. Nor were there any bombs. Nevertheless the atmosphere on board the plane remained extremely tense throughout the three-hour flight. Not because the prisoner had been eyeing the emergency exit. He was far too busy for that. Seated next to David Le Quesne, he spent some of his time studying a map of Jersey. He had not looked at the island's topography in such detail for quite some time. His eyes moved towards Grève de Lecq, an area familiar to him from his childhood. He marked the map with a dot, just a few hundred yards from Crow's Nest, the former family home since sold to the Ellams. Situated in the parish of St Ouen, it is a beautiful, rugged part of the island.

The map was handed to Paul Marks by David Le Quesne, whereupon Marks went to the back of the plane and, after a brief conversation with Roderick, took out a larger-scale map of the area. This map showed the nearby historic pub, the Moulin de Lecq, and the wooded area where Roderick and Mark had played as boys. Here too was the winding road from which he had been picked up and dropped off on his way to and from St Michael's school. He might have been absent for several years, but he knew every twist in that road, every nearby brook and bridle path, as if it had been imprinted indelibly in his mind.

Roderick made two marks on the map, indicating a strip of land on one side of the valley. Everyone then resumed their seats, Martin Fitzgerald facing the prisoner and his lawyer. All the chatter between these last two stopped and Roderick stared out of the window as they passed over northern Spain at 36,000 feet, his face a picture of despair.

'That was a very emotional moment for me,' Paul Marks recalls. 'Because it was clear that those marks indicated where the bodies of Elizabeth and Nicholas Newall were buried.'

10

The Grave at Grève de Lecq

I make this statement of my own free will. I admit
that I killed my parents at 9 Clos de l'Atlantique
on October 11th 1987. My recollection is not
completely clear after so much time. Briefly, the
circumstances were that, after Mark left, my parents and I were alone in the house and we continued talking and drinking in the sitting room. A
heated argument developed in which many old
wounds were reopened. It came to a head with my
father and I standing face to face. I told him what I
thought about him, things I had never said before.
He pushed me and I fell hitting my head on the
dining room table. I found myself near a box of my
possessions I had sorted and removed from the
attic earlier in the day. On top of the box was a
pair of rice-flails which I grabbed and used to

strike my father. I remember him falling.

My next memory was finding myself sitting on the floor of the hall. I got up and went back into the sitting room and saw my father's body. I could feel no pulse. In a complete panic, I checked the kitchen and the bedroom where I found my mother's body. It triggered a memory of also attacking her. I could find no pulse again. Then I realised I had killed both my parents. Some time later I contacted Mark and told him what had happened. I said the only thing for me to do was to kill myself. He persuaded me not to and said he would meet me at the house. When Mark arrived I think I was sitting in the lounge holding the shotgun. Mark eventually calmed me down and talked me out of taking my life.

Mark and I then took both the bodies in a hired van and buried them. We then returned to the house via La Falaise and tried to remove all traces of what had happened. My feelings of guilt and remorse have built up ever since that night. I have found it increasingly hard to live a lie. I wanted to help my uncle and aunt to end the uncertainty but I was worried about the effect on my grandmother of bringing the murder up again. I was particularly concerned for Mark who had counselled me not to take my life and who helped and supported me to come to terms with what I had done. I felt certain that the police would not accept the truth which was that he was not involved in the killings.

Soon after my arrival in Gibraltar, I instructed my lawyers to offer the police that I would return to Jersey if Mark was not prosecuted. But they made it clear that there would be no discussion along those lines. I have still not understood how I was capable of committing these horrific crimes. I think it was probably caused by the bitter childhood memories awakened by the argument. I feel relieved that this is all out in the open. I am appalled at what I did to my parents. I am very sorry that Mark is suffering when his only involvement was after the killings and to help and protect me.

It might have been the truth. But it was certainly not the whole truth. Not that that disturbed the Jersey police unduly. For finally, after years of disappointment and delay, they had got what they wanted. And remarkably speedily too, Roderick having been back on the island for barely six hours before he was signing a formal confession at Rouge Bouillon. Yet there was something they wanted still more than that telling document: the bodies of Elizabeth and Nicholas Newall.

And who better to show the police where the two victims were buried than the murderer himself? Thus, immediately after signing his statement, Roderick agreed to take police officers to identify the burial site. With the benefit of hindsight it seemed the obvious spot, within a few hundred yards of his childhood home at Grève de Lecq. For there it was that, without the slightest display of emotion, Roderick explained to the senior police officers escorting him what had happened on that fateful night six years and one month earlier. The two brothers had driven the Renault hire van down the hill of Mont de la Grève de Lecq, passed over some water piping then in place over the road, stopped the van, then rolled the bodies of their parents over a grass bank before parking the vehicle close to the Moulin de Lecq pub. Roderick had then run back up the road and crossed a field to dig the grave and bury the bodies. And yet, however familiar he might have been with that hilly, north-westerly corner of the island as a young boy, he was surprised to find on returning there that the landscape had changed considerably since 1987. As a result, he was no longer at all sure precisely where the graves might be. He pointed out to Jimmy Adamson, one of the few policemen to have been involved in the case right from the outset, five possible burial sites. In fact Roderick was exceedingly helpful in his approach, as Adamson recalls.

I knew that he was generally telling the truth. I thought that he's come so far now that there would be no point in him telling us a load of lies. It was as if he wanted to get it all off of his chest. In fact at some stages when we went to certain areas he got down and started to dig with his hands himself, as if he was going to try and find them there and then – even though he had told me that the bodies must be about three foot down because he had dug a hole about six foot in depth. So he obviously wasn't going to find the bodies – but he was like a dog digging for a bone.

With the five possible sites demarcated, the formal search was scheduled to begin the following day. Within a few hours that Sunday morning scores of police officers were waist-deep in soil as they dug for clues. Before long the entire area of Grève de Lecq looked more like an archaeological dig than a popular and picturesque tourist spot, as police screens and awnings went up and large areas of woodland were cordoned off. Peter Warren from the Jersey New Waterworks Company was called in to explain in detail what landscaping had taken place when a new pumping station had been installed; members of the public responded speedily to police appeals for old photographs of the Grève de Lecq area; Dr Gyan Fernando, Devon and Cornwall's Home Office pathologist and forensic science expert, was asked to stand by in case his expertise might be required; and both locally and nationally the atmosphere was one of intense excitement and anticipation. There was a feeling that the final mystery of the protracted Newall murder inquiry, which had simultaneously horrified and fascinated islanders since the autumn of 1987, was about to be resolved. It could surely now be only a few hours before the bodies of Elizabeth and Nicholas Newall would be unearthed. But events were not to unfold quite so smoothly.

For as darkness fell on the Monday evening, with three of the sites having yielded nothing, many of those involved in the search began to become down-hearted. An elaborate police reconstruction of conditions on the night the Newalls' bodies were buried had likewise brought no progress; nor had a subsequent visit by Roderick to Grève de Lecq assisted in any way, for he consistently pointed to the same sites. There was talk in some quarters of abandoning the entire operation. Roderick was obviously giving the police the run-around. Certainly that was Paul Marks's view:

> I was convinced that he was mucking me about. I put my arm around his shoulder at one stage in the dark and I said: 'It's a good thing I'm not your army instructor, because I wouldn't be too pleased with you, that you can't go back to the spot.' He wasn't too impressed with that comment. Because he knew that I knew that he could have taken us to the right spot on day one.

And yet there was little else for the police to do other than continue with their meticulous search. Thus day three of the search saw additional trenches dug out in site number four. When Jimmy Adamson arrived on the scene, however, fresh from a court appearance in respect of the case against Mark Newall, he was not happy that all of the area had been searched. It was Adamson's view that an additional trench ought to be dug before the police team considered moving on again. It was a hunch which was to serve him well, as he recalls.

I was digging together with PC Robbins, when we felt that the soil had changed, exactly as Roderick had explained to me. And then within minutes of that, within a couple of scoops of the soil by the mini JCB excavator, we came across what appeared to be a piece of black polythene some two foot three inches deep. We immediately stopped and I told the digger driver just to pretend to be moving some soil so as things would look natural, because the press were watching our every move. So we just carried on while Martin Fitzgerald, who was with me throughout, went across to speak to Gyan Fernando, the Home Office pathologist, to tell him that we believed we had found the bodies.

Dr Fernando was soon able to confirm the find. It had been a most dramatic moment, and one of enormous relief for all those police officers who had been investigating the case for so many years, as he recalls.

When I went down into that third trench I knew instantly that we had found the bodies. I felt round and I could feel a foot inside a shoe. It was a man's shoe and it was covered in polythene. We immediately screened the site away from the press, and decided not to use the JCB any more in case the bodies got dismembered in any way. So we started a fairly manual dig and then worked out the extent of the grave and the bodies. It took us several hours before we eventually found that there were two bodies. They were wrapped in plastic, one in blue and the other in green.

For many in the police team the feeling was one of relief and elation. Not so for Paul Marks, the man in overall charge of the operation. As for a number of police officers before him, the Newall case had come to dominate his life, often driving him nearly to distraction. By the time the bodies of Elizabeth and Nicholas Newall were being exhumed from their shabby, makeshift graves he knew very well that he was both physically and emotionally exhausted. In fact, the task of breaking the dreadful news to Stephen Newall, Nicholas's twin, came close to breaking him.

I recognized that I could no longer function properly. I felt I was losing control. Fortunately here in Jersey we have a very good system for people under stress, with immediate access to a consultant, and I took it. What got to me most was speaking to Stephen Newall, telling him that we had delivered his brother to the hospital mortuary. He was very upset indeed. And that upset me. It was a very sad sight, to see what appeared to be two people lying head to foot together, and you knew it was a husband and wife, and you knew that inside the plastic sheeting it was not going to be particularly pleasant. But it had all been very clinically done, in two separate packages.

While Paul Marks was battling with his emotions, Dr Fernando was setting up shop in the mortuary at Jersey's General Hospital in St Helier. That night he took a number of preliminary X-rays, to confirm that there were indeed two bodies and that they were human. The following day, proceeding exceedingly slowly and with the utmost care, he set about unwrapping the first body. Both bodies had been swathed in large plastic tarpaulins, probably in an attempt to prevent blood from spilling and soiling the house at Clos de L'Atlantique and the hire van. But whatever the precise motives for the painstaking wrapping-up of the bodies, it was to serve Dr Fernando's purposes well: it had been so neat and air-tight that the bodies had been very well preserved. As the pathologist would later recall:

We found various objects which definitely indicated that it was Mr Newall's body. We found quite a lot of personal belongings, and he was fully clothed – exactly as he was last seen in the Sea Crest Hotel. The most striking thing about Mr Newall's body was the good state of preservation, having been in the earth for six years. In fact the preservation was so remarkable that by looking at him I could identify him from his photographs, especially his receding hairline and distinctive features. Mrs Newall's body was in a slightly worse state.

Dr Fernando then embarked on the post-mortems, standard procedure in any murder case. Despite the passage of so much time, he had no difficulty in establishing the causes of death. For both Elizabeth and Nicholas Newall had suffered multiple injuries to their heads, with extensive lacerations measuring between one and a half and eight centimetres in length, with a series of additional fractures underlying their skulls – injuries so widespread that they were undoubtedly the cause of death. Some of the wounds inflicted on Nicholas Newall, however, appeared to be slightly different from those received by his wife – at least those to the back of his head – for they showed characteristics not exactly the same as those likely to have been caused by the pair of Chinese rice-flails which Roderick had admitted using – suggesting the use of a different weapon. Determined not to leave anything to chance, Dr Fernando took the skull of Nicholas Newall back to his laboratory in Exmouth to carry out a more detailed examination. Having carefully cleaned and reconstructed the fragments of bone, he was in little doubt that an additional weapon with a much sharper cutting edge had been used.

However ghastly the crimes committed, and whatever the precise nature of the weapons with which the Newalls had been battered and bludgeoned to death,

Roderick was now at pains to point out that he alone had murdered his parents; that his younger brother had not been responsible for the bloodshed at Clos de L'Atlantique in any way; and that Mark's role had been altogether more limited. In fact so desperate was Roderick to get his *mea culpa* message across that he took the unusual step of telephoning Jersey's Channel Television while in custody at HM Prison La Moye in order to let it be known that he was going to issue a written statement. It was absolutely imperative for it to be understood that Mark was not to blame.

> I wish to reiterate that Mark's only role in this nightmare has been to prevent me from killing myself, and by so doing to place himself in line for criminal charges. As I understand it the legal principle that governs this action is that 'no one may gain financially through criminal acts'. If Mark had wanted to gain financially his best course of action would have been to report my crime to the Police when he discovered it, gaining instantly all of my parents' estate. Instead, he put his loyalty to his brother above that of the state and as a result has destroyed a successful career and been incarcerated.

Mark, meanwhile, had been carefully keeping his own counsel. Unlike his older brother he had succeeded in keeping his mouth shut about the meal at the Sea Crest Hotel and its bloody aftermath. Silence had been his watchword; the hallmark of his approach ever since that night. Even at the moment of his dramatic arrest in Paris he had had precious little to say. Then, accompanied by a number of police officers on the short flight from France, he had simply closed his eyes when the aircraft took off, and reopened them on touching down in Jersey. A little later that day he had been similarly terse with the island's investigating officers, saying: 'I have no statement to make at this time, other than I'm not guilty of the offences that I'm charged with.'

And he had steadfastly protested his innocence ever since. But with the police dossier against him becoming ever more comprehensive and with Roderick's own version of events now in the public domain, the stance of silence was no longer tenable, as Mark knew full well. On 15 March 1994, therefore, he admitted to the police for the first time in the six-year investigation that he had been involved after all. How then had he been able to keep a straight face in front of the television cameras when, in 1987, a month or so after the disappearance of his parents, he had said: 'the chances of my parents being found alive are very slim'? How had he been able to go before Jersey's Royal Court four years later in the presumption-of-death proceedings and publicly pontificate as to what fate might have befallen his parents? The truth was that, right from the outset, as many a Jersey investigating officer had suspected, Mark had known precisely what had happened to his parents after their sumptuous last supper at the Sea Crest Hotel, for the simple reason that he had helped to bury them in the early hours of the following morning. He too had had blood on his hands.

He had been lying and perjuring himself ever since. Time at last, then, to hear Mark's own version of events. His confession read:

On the Saturday night, my brother and parents drank a great deal of alcohol. They drank champagne before they went out for dinner and several bottles of wine at dinner. On returning to the house they started on the whisky. They started to argue, not violently, about my brother's career and other matters. It was an argument I had heard before. I was sober and not interested in the argument. Therefore I went home.

Some hours later, I was contacted by Roderick. He was crying and incoherent and stated he had killed my mother and father in a drunken row and was going to kill himself. He kept saying he was sorry. I went straight to my parents' home and found my mother and father both dead. They both had serious head injuries. My brother had blood on him and was crying in a distressed state holding my father's shotgun. I told my brother that the best thing to do was to call the police. There was nobody else in the house. He said he would shoot himself. He said the police would not understand the circumstances. I argued with him for some time but I eventually agreed to help to conceal the crime. It was then, and is now, my belief that if I had not done this he would have killed himself.

I found in the boiler room, garage and garden shed, tarpaulins, tools and other equipment we used to clean the house and dispose of the bodies. I then helped him to bury the bodies in Grève de Lecq. There were several pairs of rice-flails on the floor. Roderick gathered them up and I didn't see them again. He said he had cut them up and disposed of them. I lied later to the police, my family and my friends to give my brother an alibi to cover up the crime. I am very sorry that I did not call the police that morning. I know that I made the wrong decision but at that time I could not accept the consequences that I feared of taking the matter into my own hands and calling the police. I'll always bitterly regret the pain and anguish and trouble that has been caused ever since.

11

'I Wasn't the Least Bit Surprised'

With the police unable to substantiate the murder charges against Mark, and with the brothers' confessions now apparently consistent in terms of their respective roles, it was inevitable that the capital charges against Mark would be dropped. His was the lesser role and to these revised charges he in due course pleaded guilty. He admitted that he criminally assisted Roderick after the commission of the crime in the disposal and burial of their bodies; that he assisted in the removal, destruction or concealment of the murder weapon or weapons and any other evidence of the commission of the murders, and that he made false and dishonest statements, thus assisting Roderick to evade being brought to justice.

When all of this grisly information began to emerge in public, the newspapers had a field day. 'Kung Fu

Killer' declared one of the tabloids. 'I battered my parents to death with a rice-flail', countered the *Daily Mirror*. 'Newalls Murdered with Martial Arts Weapon' said the *Jersey Evening Post*, not to be outdone. And as far as the press was concerned that seemed to conclude the matter. The explanation for the double murders seemed to be quite clear-cut. There had been a furious row between father and son. Bitter childhood memories had been triggered off, old wounds reopened during an ugly confrontation between them. But ultimately it was nothing more elaborate than a drunken brawl that had somehow managed to get out of control, with disastrous and tragic consequences for the entire family. Or was it?

For on Monday 8 August 1994, the day when the brothers finally received their formal prison sentences, the Crown sought to adduce evidence intended to demonstrate that the murders, far from being committed on the spur of the moment, had been carefully planned and premeditated. The heart of the prosecution case hinged on what came to be known as the Norman's gear. This was a reference to the most unusual package of purchases made at 11.11 a.m. at Norman's Builders Merchant in St Helier on Saturday 10 October 1987 – the day when the Newalls were due to be celebrating Elizabeth's forty-eighth birthday at a dinner at the Sea Crest Hotel – and therefore only a few hours before the murders were to take place. £103.42 had been paid in cash for two plastic tarpaulins, two spades, one torch, one lamp, batteries, two packets of red heavy duty refuse sacks, one mattock,

If the issue of the mattock is to remain a mystery, then so too must the contents of Nicholas Newall's stomach. For during the autopsies the Home Office pathologist Dr Gyan Fernando was asked by the States of Jersey police to take both liver and stomach contents from Nicholas and Elizabeth Newall. He found that both had full stomachs, indicating that they had died within four hours of their meal at the Sea Crest. But there among their mortal remains was other evidence waiting to be found. Having taken these examples for toxicology. Fernando had then forwarded the contents to another expert, Dr Alexander Allan, a forensic scientist at Aldermaston Laboratory for further screening tests. It was Allan's findings which were to become of considerable interest in the case, and in particular the presence of phenobarbitone in the liver and stomach of Nicholas Newall. Used for the treatment of epilepsy – an illness never to afflict either of the Newalls – phenobarbitone causes both drowsiness and sedation; and when taken with alcohol the dangers of overdosing are very high. But when challenged by the police that he had used phenobarbitone dissolved in whisky to drug his father prior to killing him, Roderick vigorously denied the allegation, just as he denied the use of any murder weapon other than the rice-flails. And another expert toxicologist, equally eminent and a potential witness for the defence, while accepting the presence of phenobarbitone, denied that the conclusions and inferences drawn by the prosecuting authorities were accurate and concise. It was because of these conflicting pieces of expert evidence that the issue of poisoning was quietly allowed to be dropped from the Crown case, to the fury of a number of the senior investigating officers involved.

The key issue of premeditation, therefore, was never settled in court. The defence team sought to give additional credibility to the theory of the drunken brawl, and duly cited an extract from Roderick's spontaneous confession to Helena Pedo in Brazil in which, having repeatedly branded himself as a murderer, he had pointed to a bottle of whisky and said, 'that was responsible for what happened'. The prosecution countered with an extract from Roderick's subsequent tape-recorded confession to Uncle Stephen.

'What about some mitigating circumstances, you know, like a crazy drunken rage or something. Does that mitigate your internal thing as well?'. Nicholas's identical twin had asked.

'No.' Roderick had replied.

In order to give further weight to his submission that the murders were the result of a sudden and terrible violent episode David Le Quesne then proceeded to read off a list of questions. None of the following, the Jersey Advocate argued, sounded very much like the sort of planning and preparation which one might reasonably expect from anybody contemplating the commission of such horrendous crimes, let alone an intelligent and highly trained young army officer.

'Why plan a murder in which he would inevitably be

the prime suspect; why the highly public and visible dinner at the Sea Crest Hotel; why plan a murder in such a way as to cause a blood bath; what was he planning to do with the bodies; did he really plan to drive at the dead of night right across the island; what if he had been stopped by the police; did he really plan to bury them in a place in which he would have to carry the bodies 100 yards across a meadow from the road; what if another car had passed along the road while the bodies were being dragged across the meadow; why plan to dig graves which would have to be done by torch light in a place where the torches could easily be seen from the road; why no plan for disposing of the evidence; and why have to ask a neighbour of Mark's the next day if bonfires were permitted on Noirmont Common?'

He might well have been able to come up with an equally impressive list of witnesses, had he been allowed to. But David Le Quesne informed all those present at the Royal Court that he had been specifically instructed not to attempt to excuse Roderick for his crime by indulging in character assassination of the deceased or to speak ill of the dead in any way. Having said that he nonetheless managed to include a couple of remarks gathered from Uncle Stephen himself: that Roderick and Mark were 'two very badly treated little boys', and that Mark in particular felt from an early age that his parents not only did not love him but positively disliked him.

In the event, though, not a single witness was summoned to resolve either the question of premeditation or indeed to speak highly or otherwise about the parenting meted out by the Newalls. There was thus no tense moment while a verdict was handed to Jersey's Bailiff, Sir Peter Crill, by the jury foreman. Indeed there were no jurors at all because both brothers had already pleaded guilty to their respective charges. That was not to prevent Sir Peter, however, from having his say. Passing a prison sentence of six years on Mark and two concurrent sentences of life imprisonment upon Roderick, the Bailiff reminded the brothers of the enormous gravity of their crimes, insisting to Roderick that they were particularly nasty killings. 'Over the years the crimes of patricide and matricide have attracted a particular odium.'

'The whole thing is sad, desperately sad,' laments Maureen Ellam, the current owner of Crow's Nest, the detached house perched on a hill overlooking Grève de Lecq, where the Newall boys grew up.

> Four lives have been destroyed. I still feel guilty that I didn't do more, but I didn't recognize a problem. My emotions have fluctuated considerably in relation to the boys. Despite everything I still have great sympathy with them because the young do do awful things. Elizabeth and Nicholas are dead. You can't bring them back. So do you help their children 'who know not what they do'? And then anger comes in; for Elizabeth was younger than me – and she should still be here.

The beautiful, beautiful Elizabeth, with 100 years to live. The Newalls lived life. That's why people were jealous. And thank God they did, because they both had short lives. As for me, although time does heal I hardly ever go out now – I've ended up being a hermit. But where better to be a hermit than up here at Crow's Nest?

And yet, however spectacular the views from Crow's Nest and however delightful the environs of Grève de Lecq – an enchanting blend of bay, woods and sea – Maureen Ellam knows the time has come for her to move on again.

This is the Newalls' house. It's where they spent the happiest times of their lives. It's where the boys spent their formative years. This house shrieks Newalls at you from every corner. I can't live with the pain of looking out of the window and seeing the spot where Elizabeth and Nick lay for six years without any help from me. You just can't live with such pain all of the time.

The *Star* newspaper hardly helped. For when the Newalls' bodies were being exhumed from their graves, the editor saw fit to publish a photograph of Maureen Ellam's home with the caption 'Death House'. It is hardly surprising, therefore, that the Ellams feel that they are likely to settle elsewhere.

The notion that Elizabeth and Nicholas Newall were somehow derelict in their duty as parents makes the blood of Stephen Newall rise rapidly to boiling point. For as the press and public dwelled on the details of the boys' upbringing, attempting to paint a picture of deprivation and neglect, had it not become obvious that the tables had turned, with the victims themselves having ended up on trial and in the dock?

A lot of what has been said and written about my brother, including in this book, is absolute nonsense. Warts have been blown up into balloons; they have been presented as horrible people, which they were not. I do feel very strongly that the good name of my brother, who was just an ordinary chap, has been blackened and besmirched. A lot of bizarre nonsenses and blatant half-truths have been written and recorded which people are likely to accept simply because Elizabeth and Nicholas have no way of being able to speak up for themselves. That is ridiculously and grotesquely unfair. Why doesn't anyone ever print the positive things about them? Come up to Scotland and hear how highly they were thought of up here. You can say what you like about the boys, but their parents were good people who died in tragic circumstances. That's the real message which should be coming across.

Nan Clark, Elizabeth's sister, has a slightly different perspective. Her overriding concern has been to be able to produce a satisfactory answer to one simple question, something which has always eluded her.

Ever since she realized that her nephews were much more deeply involved in the case than they were letting on to the police, this riddle has preyed on her mind.

Why? If the boys were sitting here I would just want to say 'why'? I often wonder where we went wrong. It all seemed fine to me watching them grow up. Where did we fail? How did communications break down so disastrously? I just want them to talk to me about what is really important; not stuff on the periphery. So that I can come to understand what it is all about. Because it's so frustrating not to know. From time to time Mark will ring me up from prison and of course neither of us ever mentions the fact that he helped to bury my sister, that he lied to the police for year after year, and that together with Roderick he has caused the most awful suffering and sorrow. So sometimes I have to pinch myself to remind myself what has happened; it's like being on the other side of the looking glass.

Exceptionally close to Elizabeth, Nan Clark has been unable or unwilling to bring herself to bid her sister a final farewell.

Because the person that she was has become part of me. Our friends are still alive. I used to shop a lot for Elizabeth, especially for clothes. It has been very difficult to stop myself looking on dress rails

235

for her too. Or then someone might get off a bus; I would think it was her. I like to talk about her and think about her. I just can't believe that she is no longer part of my life. Maybe that will come after the funeral, I don't know. But I have missed her and do miss her very much. You can say anything to a sister; we were very honest together. And the manner of her death was so terribly horrifying. Nor will this tragedy ever end for our family. For how is the future going to be tenable for us? In a family where one boy has murdered his parents and the other helped to clear up and bury them? This tragedy will never end for us, even when I die. Because my own boys will in due course have to get on with Roderick and Mark, their cousins; they might even wish one day to become involved in running the family's paint business in Scotland, where we have a £4 million per year turnover, perhaps even taking a seat on the board. So one way or another we will be dealing with this for as long as I can imagine.

So many lives, then, affected by the Newall case. So many questions still to be answered. Nor has the States of Jersey police force ever experienced anything on the scale of the Newall inquiry. During the course of the six-year investigation, officers took no fewer than 790 statements; pursued 2890 lines of inquiry; produced 2904 documents and conducted interviews with thousands of people in almost a dozen countries spanning three continents. It was all a far cry from the summer shoplifting season in St Helier. The FBI had become involved, the Ministry of Defence, police surveillance teams, army search advisers, and countless other official agencies. Directly or indirectly, almost every officer within the force's 232 men and women had become part of the case, with a wide range of independent experts offering advice and assistance as and when more specialist help was required. Thus it was that a series of archaeologists, pathologists, odontologists, entomologists, toxicologists and geologists – to list but a few – came to write up records and reports on the case. Millions of pounds were spent; special budgets voted upon and approved; millions of miles travelled. But ultimately it was teamwork which was to provide the key to success, as Paul Marks explains:

Bringing criminals to justice should be a straightforward affair. This case, with all its twists and turns, made mincemeat of the process. Nevertheless, with collaboration between the police forces of the world, an alliance with those responsible for prosecuting the case, particularly Desmond de Silva QC for his work in Gibraltar and the assistance of a multitude of expert witnesses, a semblance of order was achieved.

Without witnesses, and there were many, and without the co-operation, however harrowing, of members of the family of Nicholas and Elizabeth, these foul crimes would not have been

237

brought before the courts.

Some would say that a larger force would have cracked this case long ago; I say not so. You would have to go a long way to find a community and the police force it serves so committed and willing to back that commitment with the funds needed to conclude an inquiry of this type. I have a message for the whole world: Jersey is the last place to commit such crimes and long may it remain so.

It might well have ended in victory. But the Newall case had the Jersey police foxed for a good many years. For despite all the effort and expense the brothers had come within a hair's breadth of getting away with it. They had been free, leading the good life, working, travelling, sailing, jetting and playing around the world. Everybody knew that the Jersey police suspected the brothers. But throughout the late eighties and beyond, the law-enforcement agencies had been unable to gather sufficient evidence to feel confident of bringing a successful prosecution against them. It was as simple as that. Nor had they ever really been able to come up with anything concrete in respect of the complex issue of motive.

Not so Angela Barnes, the woman who had greeted the Newall family almost from the very moment of their arrival in Jersey some twenty years before the couple died. More than any other person on the island, she had come to know the Newalls well. She knew all about motive.

It was just a matter of time. This deed was waiting to be done. It was the lack of love. I knew that Roderick had attacked his mother in the past. I had seen the bitter rows, the dire threats and fighting for myself. Some of it had even taken place within my home. So my closing comment on the whole sorry story is this – that when Elizabeth and Nicholas were murdered, I wasn't the least bit surprised.

More True Crime from Headline:

ROCKY STOCKMAN
—— THE ——
HANGMAN'S DIARY

A CALENDAR OF
JUDICIAL HANGINGS
Introduction by Colin Wilson

**An extraordinary calendar of judicial hangings from around
the world and through the ages…**

3 January
1946 THE END OF LORD HAW-HAW
William Joyce (40), dubbed 'Lord Haw-Haw', hanged at Wandsworth Prison for
treason. *Hangman: Albert Pierrepoint*

23 February
1885 THE 'MAN THEY COULD NOT HANG'
John Lee (19) was the 'Man They Could Not Hang' at Exeter Gaol. He had been
sentenced for the murder of his employer Emma Keyse (68). *Hangman: James Berry*

28 May
1686 HANGMAN HANGED
Pascha Rose, butcher and public hangman, hanged at Tyburn Tree for housebreaking and theft. *Hangman: Jack Ketch*

19 August
1692 SALEM WITCHES
Reverend George Burroughs (42), and others, hanged at Gallows Hill, Salem,
Massachusetts, USA, for witchcraft. *Hangman: Sheriff John Corwin*

23 November
1910 'THE MURDER OF THE CENTURY'
Dr Hawley Harvey Crippen (48) hanged at Pentonville Prison for the murder and
dismemberment of his wife Cora Crippen (37). *Hangman: John Ellis*

24 December
1867 THE MURDER AND MUTILATION OF SWEET FANNY ADAMS
Frederick Baker (29) publicly hanged at Winchester Prison for the ghastly murder
of Fanny Adams (8). *Hangman: William Calcraft*

NON-FICTION/TRUE CRIME   0 7472 4015 9

THE UFO ENCYCLOPEDIA

THE MOST COMPREHENSIVE BOOK ON UFOLOGY EVER WRITTEN

COMPILED AND EDITED BY

JOHN SPENCER

FOR THE BRITISH UFO RESEARCH ASSOCIATION

Compiled by one of the world's leading authorities
on the subject, THE UFO ENCYCLOPEDIA is an
authoritative, level-headed and witty reference book
covering all aspects of the UFO phenomenon.
It includes:

* Over 1,000 entries and over 70 colour and black
and white photos

* In-depth analyses of celebrated cases including the
Gulf Breeze Sightings, the Pascagoula Abduction
and the Trindade Island photographs

* First-hand accounts of alien abductions

* Rare photographs and previously unknown cases

* The latest information on related phenomena
including corn circles and the Bermuda Triangle

THE UFO ENCYCLOPEDIA

- a comprehensive manual for professionals and
amateurs alike.

NON-FICTION/REFERENCE   0 7472 3494 9

A selection of non-fiction from Headline

THE *INDEPENDENT* BOOK OF ANNIVERSARIES	George Beal	£8.99 ☐
MEAN BEANS	Cas Clarke	£5.99 ☐
ENCYCLOPEDIA OF FORENSIC SCIENCE	Brian Lane	£7.99 ☐
JUST THE ONE: The Wives and Times of Jeffrey Bernard	Graham Lord	£6.99 ☐
MALE SEXUAL AWARENESS	Barry McCarthy	£5.99 ☐
BURNS: A Biography of Robert Burns	James Mackay	£8.99 ☐
WORLD ENCYCLOPEDIA OF 20TH CENTURY MURDER	Jay Robert Nash	£8.99 ☐
PLAYFAIR FOOTBALL ANNUAL 1993-94	Jack Rollin (Ed)	£3.99 ☐
HEART AND SOLE	David Sole with Derek Douglas	£5.99 ☐

All Headline books are available at your local bookshop or newsagent, or can be ordered direct from the publisher. Just tick the titles you want and fill in the form below. Prices and availability subject to change without notice.

Headline Book Publishing PLC, Cash Sales Department, Bookpoint, 39 Milton Park, Abingdon, OXON, OX14 4TD, UK. If you have a credit card you may order by telephone – 0235 831700.

Please enclose a cheque or postal order made payable to Bookpoint Ltd to the value of the cover price and allow the following for postage and packing:
UK & BFPO: £1.00 for the first book, 50p for the second book and 30p for each additional book ordered up to a maximum charge of £3.00.
OVERSEAS & EIRE: £2.00 for the first book, £1.00 for the second book and 50p for each additional book.

Name ....

Address ....

....

....

If you would prefer to pay by credit card, please complete:
Please debit my Visa/Access/Diner's Card/American Express (delete as applicable) card no:

Signature .... Expiry Date ....